D1053360

SELF-DRIVING CARS

THE NEW WAY FORWARD

MICHAEL FALLON

TWENTY-FIRST CENTURY BOOKS / MINNEAPOLIS

Twenty-First Century Books
A division of Lerner Publishing Group, Inc.
241 First Avenue North
Minneapolis, MN 55401 USA

For reading levels and more information, look up this title at www.lernerbooks.com.

Main body text set in Avenir LT Std 11/15
Typeface provided by Adobe Systems.

Library of Congress Cataloging-in-Publication Data

Names: Fallon, Michael, 1966– author.
Title: Self-driving cars : the new way forward / Michael Fallon.
Description: Minneapolis, MN : Twenty-First Century Books, [2018] | Includes
    bibliographical references and index. | Audience: Ages 13-18. | Audience:
    Grade 9 to 12. |
Identifiers: LCCN 2017043700 (print) | LCCN 2018002936 (ebook) |
    ISBN 9781541524835 (eb pdf) | ISBN 9781541500556 (lb : alk. paper)
Subjects: LCSH: Autonomous vehicles—History. | Automobiles—Automatic
    control—History. | Automobile industry and trade—Technological
    innovations.
Classification: LCC TL152.8 (ebook) | LCC TL152.8 .F35 2018 (print) | DDC 629.2-
    -dc23

LC record available at https://lccn.loc.gov/2017043700

Manufactured in the United States of America
1-43698-33490-2/1/2018

CONTENTS

WHEN TRANSPORTATION TECHNOLOGIES COLLIDE

In the late nineteenth century, the small factory town of Westfield, Massachusetts, was known around the nation as Whip City. Westfield had been founded in the 1660s as a farming community. In the nineteenth century, new industries transformed the town's economy. Companies in Westfield made popular products such as bicycles, boilers, bricks, cigars, machinery, paper products, radiators, wood products, and more. Most important among these products were parts and tools for the most common forms of transportation at the time: buggies, carriages, coaches, and horse-drawn carts.

The American Whip Company (*pictured here in 1891*) and several other companies made Westfield, Massachusetts, a hub for the manufacturing of buggy whips. These whips, used to direct horse-drawn vehicles, were a common item in the era before car-based transportation.

In 1895 thirty-seven separate factories in Westfield made buggy whips. Drivers of horse-drawn vehicles used these whips to urge their horses to move faster or to slow their pace. By 1900 Whip City's whip factories produced 99 percent of the world's supply of buggy whips. Westfield's thriving local economy provided the community with money to build a beautiful town hall, several libraries, high-quality public schools, and a tree-lined downtown area with paved sidewalks. But Westfield's reign as Whip City did not last. By 1926, with radically new inventions in transportation, all but one of Westfield's thirty-seven whip factories had closed.

And the development that caused this dramatic change? A new technology called the automobile.

WHIP CITY

Westfield, Massachusetts, is still known as Whip City. But of the thirty-seven factory buildings that once stood in Whip City, only four are still standing. The National Register of Historic Places includes all four, and most serve new purposes. The Sanford Whip Factory building, for instance, offers affordable housing. The H. M. Van Deusen Whip Company is an apartment building, and the United States Whip Company Complex is a shopping center. The Westfield Whip Manufacturing Company, founded in 1887, is the only factory that continues to make whips. They are sold mostly to collectors.

The American Whip Company (*left*), in 1879, later known as the United States Whip Company, once produced buggy whips for horse-drawn vehicles. After changes in driving technology and other areas of US culture, the building serves as a shopping complex (*below*).

A SLOW EMERGENCE

The technology that became the automobile took centuries to develop. In 1478 the famous Italian designer, artist, and engineer Leonardo da Vinci drew plans for a self-propelled cart that moved according to a series of complex spring mechanisms. The design perplexed people, since they did not understand how springs could provide forward motion. Several years later, da Vinci described in his notebooks another propelled device, called the Architonnerre. Although da Vinci did not build this device in his lifetime, his design included a machine using compressed steam to fire a projectile through a metal tube.

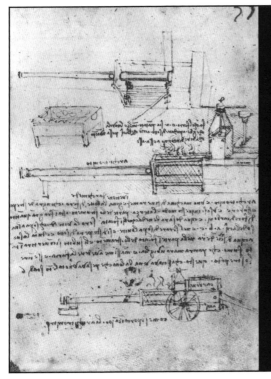

Around the year 1500, artist and inventor Leonardo da Vinci produced a pen-and-ink drawing for a device known as the Architonnerre. His design anticipated elements of the technology later used to create the automobile. Scholars examining the design have determined that da Vinci envisioned the Architonnerre using the power of compressed steam to propel a projectile forward.

Two centuries later, inventors designed another technology that used steam to create motion: the steam engine. The steam engine of 1712, developed by English inventor Thomas Newcomen, was an early form of internal combustion engine. Internal combustion engines burn fuel in confined spaces called combustion chambers. The resulting hot gases expand in the chamber, putting pressure on pistons (disks or cylinders) or rotors (a hub) to move the shafts to which they are connected. This process turns the wheels of an automobile. Most modern automobiles use a more advanced version of this type of engine.

In 1769 Nicolas Joseph Cugnot of France built the first working, self-propelled, land-based mechanical vehicle. A steam engine powered Cugnot's vehicle. Both the Automobile Club of France and the British Royal Automobile Club recognize it as the world's first automobile. Other historians argue that, in 1808, François Isaac de Rivaz of France built the first true internal-combustion automobile. His vehicle used a hydrogen-powered internal combustion engine with an electric ignition.

Neither of these innovators was commercially successful, however. Then came the Industrial Revolution. Starting between 1760 and 1780, manufacturing in factories began to replace home-based manufacturing. Instead of making one thing at a time by hand, workers could rely on mechanical equipment and steam power to produce multiple copies of a single product quickly. By the 1830s and 1840s, the new industrial practices had transformed daily life in many nations. Manufactured goods became cheaper and more widespread, and

Many historians consider the *fardier à vapeur* (steam dray, or vehicle to haul goods) to be the first self-propelled land vehicle. In 1769 Nicolas Joseph Cugnot built the first *fardier à vapeur*. In 1770 he built a second, larger version, seen here at the Musée des Arts et Métiers in Paris, France.

standards of living improved for the general population. In 1885 Karl Benz in Germany developed the Benz Patent-Motorwagen, the first successful production automobile—a vehicle design of which a manufacturer makes more than one exact copy. Benz was the first to sell these production automobiles commercially. He produced and sold twenty-five of the Patent-Motorwagen between 1886 and 1895.

At first, the public didn't take these automobiles seriously. People called them horseless carriages, or

Karl Benz (*seated, center*) created the Benz Patent-Motorwagon (*above*), the first production automobile. Benz sold more than two dozen of the Benz Patent-Motorwagen between 1886 and 1895.

gasoline buggies, and saw them as rattling pieces of machinery that broke down too often and caused more trouble than they were worth. Some people feared for their safety in and around early automobiles. Others laughed at stories of motorists stranded on remote highways while travelers in horse-drawn vehicles arrived at home safe and sound.

By the late nineteenth century and early twentieth century, cities and towns across the United States had built a large number of roads specially designed for people traveling by horse and buggy or by bicycle. Automobiles were often ill suited to these roads.

IRKSOME CHANGE

Thorstein Veblen (1857–1929, *below*), an American sociologist, documented the rapid societal changes of the late nineteenth century. He argued that most humans prefer customs and traditions to progress and social change. In his 1899 book *The Theory of the Leisure Class,* Veblen commented on people's reluctance to accept modern machinery. He noted that "all change in habits of life and of thought is irksome." He also suggested that human

nature contains "an instinctive revulsion at any departure from the accepted way of doing and of looking at things." These observations may help explain why the people of Veblen's era at first resisted the automobile.

They were too narrow and winding for the difficult-to-control contraptions. The vehicles competed for space on city streets with horse-drawn carriages and bicycles.

Suspicions about the safety and reliability of automobiles lingered into the early twentieth century, and buggy whips seemed certain to remain a necessity. At the same time, the industrial strength of the United States was growing, as was the spending power of individual Americans. Consumer culture began to emerge in the United States during the 1910s and the 1920s. For the first time, Americans had a wide range of manufactured consumer goods to choose from. They had well-made industrial goods such as household appliances, factory-made clothing, and new inventions including the electric phonograph, the electric vacuum cleaner, and commercial radios. This cultural shift would soon cross over into the field of transportation.

SPEEDING THINGS UP

In the early twentieth century, automobile manufacturing was slow and costly. Assembling cars required the skills of master crafters who carefully fitted parts together to make an entire automobile. As a result, the first automobiles were too expensive for most people to buy. For example, in 1909 the German car manufacturer Daimler-Motoren-Gesellschaft (DMG) employed seventeen hundred workers in its factories and produced fewer than one thousand cars during the year. The DMG model, called the Mercedes Simplex, was then considered the most technologically advanced automobile. It was the most reliable and the fastest car of its time. However, because the factory could only

Manufacturing the first automobiles was expensive and time intensive. Few consumers were able to purchase the end result. But with the innovations of Henry Ford, automobiles became more affordable. In this photo from the early 1900s, identical parts of a Ford Model T vehicle travel down an assembly line.

produce a few Mercedes Simplexes over a long period, the car's price tag was very high. In 1909 the Simplex cost between $7,000 and $8,000 (the equivalent of about $192,332 to $219,808 in the twenty-first century). Only the wealthiest people could purchase these automobiles.

As the nineteenth century ended and a new century began, the purchasing power of consumers in the United States—and the demand for new products—continued to grow. US factories pushed to create products faster and cheaper. And in the world of automobiles, a Michigan native named Henry Ford explored new innovations.

Ford had become interested in automobiles as a young man, while working as an engineer for the Edison Illuminating Company in Detroit. In 1896, as a hobby, Ford built his own horseless carriage, which he called the quadricycle, in a shed behind his home.

In 1899 Ford started a small business called the Detroit Automotive Company where he worked to improve his original quadricycle. However, his partners in the company grew frustrated with Ford's constant tinkering. They wanted him to produce a product they could sell as soon as possible. In 1902 Ford left the

The Ford Motor Company released its first Model T vehicle in 1908. The vehicle had a lower price than the products of Ford's competitors. In 1913 Ford began using a moving assembly line to manufacture its cars. This led to even lower prices and more consumers adopting automobiles.

company. (It then became the Cadillac Automobile Company.) In 1903 he founded a new business: the Ford Motor Company.

Ford's first automobile—the Model A—went on sale a few months after Ford Motor Company opened. As with other car factories, production was slow at the Ford factory. The company only assembled a few Model A automobiles each day. Henry Ford dedicated himself to producing automobiles faster and cheaper. In 1908 Ford released a new car, the Model T. The first Model T was much cheaper than other automobiles, costing $825 in 1908 (or around $22,669 in twenty-first-century dollars). "When I'm through," he famously said of the Model T, "everybody will have one."

Within a few days of the launch of the Model T, Americans had placed fifteen thousand orders for the automobile. In fact, the Ford Motor Company received more orders than it could fill. Ford began to reexamine the methods that his factories used to build the cars. Eventually, he struck on an innovative idea.

On December 1, 1913, Ford Motor Company installed the first moving assembly line in its factory. The assembly line moved standardized, interchangeable parts along a track to different assembly points. At each assembly point, a laborer quickly performed a specific assembly task, and then the car moved on to the next point. Instead of using master crafters to make entire cars, this quick and efficient means of production relied on many workers to build a single car. It reduced the time to build a car from more than twelve hours to two and one-half hours. As a result, the price of the Model T dropped. By 1925 a Model T cost just $290 (or about $4,103 in twenty-first-century dollars). This was less than three months' wages for the average American worker.

DOMINATING THE ROADS

By the time Ford Motor Company stopped producing the Model T in 1927, the company had sold more than 16.5 million vehicles. By then other factories around the world had started using Ford's assembly-line methods to make affordable automobiles. So, by the 1930s, automobiles had become the most widely used form of transportation in the world. Once an object of suspicion and ridicule, automobiles were too appealing to ignore. People could go almost any place they wanted in a car. And they could get there two or three times faster than in any other form of transportation. But challenges lay ahead.

The Great Depression (1929–1942) was a devastating global economic downturn. Banks failed, factories closed, and millions of Americans lost their jobs and their homes. They no longer had money to buy cars and other extras. The sale of automobiles shrank from more than two million cars in 1928 to less than one million in 1932. Then, in 1941, the United States entered World War II (1939–1945). During wartime, much of American industry shifted from the production of consumer goods such as cars and appliances to the production of weapons and other supplies for military personnel. Resources such as gasoline, leather, meat, rubber, and wool were rationed—civilians could buy only limited amounts of them.

The United States and its allies won the war. Industries boomed in the late 1940s and the 1950s, and Americans once again had money to spend. Factories turned out cars in great numbers. While US auto manufacturers had built only around 1.1 million cars in 1942, in 1946 the number increased to 3.2 million and continued to increase through the late 1940s and early 1950s. Automobiles became a symbol of growing prosperity in the United States. With their new mobility, many Americans left the inner cities and moved into the nation's new suburbs. And with more leisure time, they piled into the family car to take road vacations to places they had always wanted to see.

In the 1950s, the automobile became a larger part of US culture and a symbol of prosperity. Advertising of the time reflected this development, positioning automobiles as a central part of the American dream.

The growth of the automobile industry caused an economic revolution across the United States. Many factories that produced older technologies such as horse-drawn vehicles and buggy whips closed. Dozens of other industries opened or expanded. The demand grew for vulcanized rubber, which made car tires more durable. New rubber factories emerged to meet the demand. Steel plants produced steel for the frames, bodies, and engine parts of cars, and oil companies produced gasoline to power the cars. The need for building new roads, highways, parking lots, and service stations created thousands of new jobs. Numerous people also began to make their living by fixing automobiles. And motor hotels, or motels, opened along highways next to roadside diners, providing lodging and food for cross-country drivers.

CAR-BASED CULTURE

The large-scale shift to cars as the United States' main form of transportation created a car-based culture in the country. It forever changed the ways Americans live, work, travel, and spend their spare time. Many forms of business—such as raising crops and transporting goods—rely on automobiles, tractors, construction vehicles, and large big rig trucks. Cars also determine how Americans organize their cities, suburbs, and other public spaces.

Gas stations, parking ramps and underground lots, roadways and freeways, overpasses and on-ramps, tollbooths, and rest stops fill huge tracts of land across the United States. Experts estimate that a city such as Los Angeles, California, uses as much as two-thirds of its land to support cars. Automobiles are also at the root of numerous quality-of-life issues in US culture. These included suburban sprawl, dense traffic congestion and air pollution in cities, and drive-through fast-food restaurants and the related increase in obesity.

Producing and consuming gasoline has even more serious consequences for humans worldwide. Cars and other vehicles that run on fossil fuels such as gasoline and diesel release huge amounts of carbon exhaust, contributing to global warming and climate change. Global warming is the increase of trapped heat in Earth's atmosphere, which leads to climate change—the change in weather patterns around the planet. Many policy makers, health officials, and drivers believe that the current transportation system in the United States and elsewhere should be replaced with a more Earth-friendly model.

As early as the 1930s, not long after the age of the automobile had dawned, theorists and designers began to imagine a better kind of automobile. They envisioned a car that would offer the freedom and convenience that people want but with fewer of the drawbacks. In the 1980s and 1990s, research institutes and automobile companies got serious. They began to think about new car designs with constructive disruptive technology. This concept advocates applying radically new car innovations (disruptions) in a useful or constructive way and to improve upon existing transportation systems.

These innovations include integrating more safety features in car designs and using computer-processing technology for the systems that run automobiles. They also include cleaner and environmentally friendly electric and hybrid-electric engines. The research has also taken self-driving cars from a possibility to a certainty.

CHAPTER ONE

THE ORIGINS OF THE SELF-DRIVING CAR

The idea of a self-driving automobile dates back to the 1920s, when cars were becoming a mass technology. In 1925 an engineer named Francis P. Houdina developed the means to direct a car using radio signals. Houdina attached an antenna to a 1926 Chandler automobile to control the car's steering wheel, accelerator, and brakes. On July 27, 1925, the Houdina Radio Control Company held a demonstration on the streets of New York City. As crowds gathered, an employee of the company followed behind the remote-control car to keep it on course.

Houdina's demonstration was a failure. The remote-control operator lost control of the Chandler. According to a *New York Times* report the next day, "The radio car careened from left to right, down Broadway, around

Designer Norman Bel Geddes brought the Futurama exhibit to the 1939 World's Fair in New York City. This exhibit put Bel Geddes's dream of a safe, efficient, autonomous (self-directing) highway on display for fairgoers.

Columbus Circle, and south on Fifth Avenue, almost running down two trucks and a milk wagon, which took to the curbs for safety." Francis Houdina himself lunged for the remote-control car's steering wheel. He was unable to prevent the car from crashing into the fender of an automobile filled with photographers. The police eventually ordered Houdina to stop his demonstration.

Self-driving technology remained elusive in the following decades. But the idea continued to intrigue people. Industrial designer Norman Bel Geddes became famous in 1939 for Futurama, an exhibit he designed for that year's World's Fair in New York City. The exhibit was a scale model of a future city that presented a possible vision for what the world would look like in twenty years.

Among Bel Geddes's chief ideas was a new national system of expressways to promote a free flow of people and goods across the country. He also imagined the widespread use of a new and efficient type of power plant, individual flying machines, and autonomous (self-driving) automobiles. To give visitors a glimpse of this technology-driven future, he produced a vast (0.3-mile, or 0.5 km) scale model of his vision for the country. Fairgoers traveled above the model on a moving conveyer belt and examined its wonders through a curved pane of glass.

> "INCREASING FREEDOM OF MOVEMENT MAKES POSSIBLE A MAGNIFICENTLY FULL, RICH LIFE FOR THE PEOPLE OF OUR TIME."
>
> —Norman Bel Geddes, *Magic Motorways*

THE MAGIC MOTORWAY WILL CURE WHAT AILS US

The next year, Bel Geddes published a book called *Magic Motorways*. In it, he described a national system of radio-controlled electric cars propelled by electromagnetic fields (a field of force that an electric charge produces by interacting with magnetic components). Bel Geddes believed the realities of driving had come to frustrate drivers. In *Magic Motorways*, he wrote that people felt "harassed by the daily task of getting from one place to another, by the nuisances of intersectional jams, narrow, congested bottlenecks, dangerous night driving, annoying policemen's whistles, honking horns, blinking traffic lights, confusing highway signs, and irritating traffic regulations." Most of all, he added, people were appalled by the daily toll of highway accidents and deaths. They were "eager to find a sensible way out of this planless, suicidal mess."

A smooth-working system of self-driving cars, Bel Geddes argued, would free human drivers from the burden of driving. It would also eliminate the human error that caused auto-related accidents, harm, and death. His autonomous highway system of self-driving cars, he wrote, was designed "to make automobile collisions impossible and to eliminate traffic congestion."

Throughout the book, Bel Geddes expanded on his vision for a national highway system and for the self-driving cars that would use it. His automatically controlled motorway would follow four basic principles of highway design: safety, comfort, speed, and economy. To meet these principles, a controlling device, not human drivers, would propel automobiles on the motorway. The cars would travel in individual lanes bordered by electromagnetic separators.

The details of the technology for the car's controlling device were somewhat sketchy. Bel Geddes proposed a cog track. This slotted track would be set into the road, and cars would be fitted with cogwheels that connected with the track and propelled the car forward. For safety, the system would move the cars forward at a set speed and at a set distance between all the cars.

If that technology failed to emerge, Bel Geddes proposed using electromagnetic forces not only to separate the lanes but also to control the automobiles. In the 1930s, scientists were developing new ways to run a current of electricity through a magnet to increase the force of magnetic attraction. At the time, these researchers believed that magnetic attraction could power motor vehicles. Scientists eventually realized that the system would require too many electromagnets to produce enough energy.

Still, the highway system that Bel Geddes envisioned had some advantages. In his model, each self-driving car would travel in its lane at a controlled speed, with none of the dangerous variations in speed that could lead to accidents. To move their car out of a lane and into another, passengers would press a button on an instrument panel. Sensors would minimize the possibility of a collision by making sure the car shifted lanes only if it could remain at a safe distance from the other cars in that lane. Control towers along the highway every 5 miles (8 km) or so would help maintain order and avoid any obstacles to safe, comfortable, and speedy travel.

VISION AND REALITY

Norman Bel Geddes's vision for a safe, autonomous highway was compelling. So compelling, in fact, that in 1939, President Franklin Delano Roosevelt invited him to the White House to discuss building such a system.

The United States' involvement in World War II curtailed the growth of car-based culture in North America. Gasoline rationing required people to drive less often and more efficiently.

Bel Geddes predicted that the United States would implement his system, or something like it, by 1960. But it didn't happen that way. In 1941, shortly after the publication of Bel Geddes's *Magic Motorways*, the United States entered World War II. The nation focused all its technological innovations on the war effort—designing and building tanks, bombers, and other military equipment—not new civilian transportation systems. The strict rationing of gasoline also temporarily reduced the use of automobiles among civilians.

After World War II, US industry shifted from producing goods for war to goods for American consumers. The United States grew into the world's largest producer and user of automobiles. Ford and Chevrolet (a division of General Motors)—the United States' two largest car manufacture's in the mid-twentieth century—went from producing about 400,000 cars in 1942 to more than 2.7 million cars in 1950. Two other divisions of General Motors, Cadillac and Oldsmobile, experienced similar growth. However, the US road system was unable to handle the rapidly increasing number of cars.

In 1956 President Dwight D. Eisenhower signed into law the $25 billion Federal-Aid Highway Act (also known as the National Interstate and Defense Highways Act). Eisenhower had served as a military general during World War II, and he believed that a modern highway system would be good for national defense. He also realized a "safe and adequate" highway system would be good for citizens and for commerce. Roadbuilding crews set to work to construct the interstate highway system, which grew to include 42,793 miles (68,868 km) of US highways.

This system spurred economic growth around the country and connected isolated regions and people. It also led to more automobile congestion and the decline of the national railway system and other forms of mass transit. Locally owned mom-and-pop businesses were replaced with chain stores and restaurants. Suburbs grew at the expense of rural areas and inner cities, which lost residents, businesses, and the revenue from taxes that came with them. With more cars on the road, air quality declined because of increasing automobile emissions.

A CENTURY OF SMOG

In the late 1940s and early 1950s, people around the world became increasingly aware of the dangers of car-created air pollution. In Los Angeles, California, which had struggled with air-quality problems since the early twentieth century, smog alerts became such a normal part of life that the city was dubbed the smog capital of America. In 1959 Los Angeles authorities reported that smog caused widespread eye irritation among residents on 187 days of the year. In 1962 the number of eye-irritation days in Los Angeles had grown to 212. The increasing number of automobiles and the growth in automobile emissions through the twentieth century have forced people to seek ways to deal with worsening air quality. In the Los Angeles of the twenty-first century, air quality continues to be a concern, despite the city's emission standards for diesel trucks, gas-burning engines, and coal-fired power plants, which are some of the world's strictest.

During the 1940s, air-quality concerns became a part of everyday life in Los Angeles, California.

Even more worrisome was the increase in auto-accident fatalities.

Because of these problems, several large American corporations took a second look at whether a safer, more efficient system of roads and automobiles was possible.

"SELECTING YOUR LANE, YOU SETTLE BACK TO ENJOY THE RIDE AS YOUR CAR ADJUSTS ITSELF TO THE PRESCRIBED SPEED. YOU MAY PREFER TO READ OR CARRY ON A CONVERSATION WITH YOUR PASSENGERS—OR EVEN TO CATCH UP ON YOUR OFFICE WORK. . . . FANTASTIC? NOT AT ALL."

—*Electronic Age*, January 1958

For example, in 1956, General Motors (GM) showed a film called *Key to the Future* at its annual Motorama touring festival, which traveled to five cities throughout that year. The film reintroduced ideas from Bel Geddes's Futurama exhibit, moving the date for when automation could become reality from 1960 to 1976. GM's ideas included a safe, fast-moving, futuristic highway without traffic jams or traffic fatalities. GM cars would have a screen showing details about the conditions of the roads and the best routes to take. A safety lane in every highway system would offer passengers an automatic control option, and control towers would send signals to keep cars safe and on their routes.

HIGHWAY OF THE FUTURE

By 1958 more than sixty-seven million cars were registered in the United States, more than twice the number at the start of the decade. That year the January issue of the Radio Corporation of America (RCA) magazine *Electronic Age* described a vision of the "highway of the future" that sounded a lot like the ideas of GM and Bel Geddes. The magazine article said, "You reach over to your dashboard and push the button marked 'Electronic Drive.' Selecting your lane, you settle back to enjoy the ride as your car adjusts itself to the prescribed speed. You may prefer to read or carry on a conversation with your passengers—or even to catch up on your office work. It makes no difference for the next several hundred miles as far as the driving is concerned. Fantastic? Not at all."

In fact, just two months before the magazine article came out, RCA engineers had built a test portion of the automatic highway that *Electronic Age* described. They used a 400-foot (122 m) strip of public highway on the outskirts of Lincoln, Nebraska, for their testing space. The engineers had built a test car with equipment designed to receive electrical signals from electronic circuits buried within wires in the pavement. The signals controlled the car's steering and braking to keep it in its lane. The signals also warned of obstructions ahead (such as roadwork or a stalled vehicle). The car would drive with nonautomated cars, so it also delivered an automatic warning signal to drivers in nonautomated cars that were following too closely. Besides those features, a series of lights along the sides of the highway signaled to the car's sensors when the vehicle was approaching an intersection or any other section of road where it might meet other vehicles.

Nearly one hundred state and federal highway officials, car-manufacturer representatives, and journalists were present for the RCA test. It was not without flaws, however. At one point, a driver had to disengage the car's automatic-pilot system to avoid slamming into a car ahead of it. The driver later claimed he had forgotten to flip a switch.

After the tests, RCA engineers boldly predicted that their vision for a system of automated electronic highways would become a reality by 1975, one year before GM's prediction. In 1960, working with GM, RCA built and demonstrated a larger version of its highway of the future on a test track in Princeton, New Jersey. Once again, RCA's engineers buried electronic cables in the road and added sensors to the front bumpers of their test car to detect information about road conditions. The engineers replaced the steering wheel and pedals on the test car with a small joystick and an emergency brake. A meter on the dashboard displayed the car's speed as well as the distance to any cars in front of the self-driving car.

These RCA demonstrations were not successful from a publicity standpoint. In a newspaper account of the New Jersey test, one witness wrote, "[The author] Washington Irving put the headless horseman [the ghost of a soldier] on paper [in his story "The Legend of Sleepy Hollow"]. A corporation named RCA now has put the driverless car on the road. The automation tends to be as scary as [Irving's] ghost, until you get used to it. But someday we may have to live with it." The fact that a driver was forced to take over manual control of the car to avoid a collision, along with reporters' less-than-glowing descriptions, raised fears among the American public. Self-driving technology would have to be almost flawless before drivers would give up control of their cars. Bold predictions for a fully autonomous highway system by 1975 did not pan out.

DANGERS ON THE ROAD

Between 1920 and 1965, the number of registered vehicles (cars and trucks) on roads in the United States increased from 7.5 million to 91.7 million. Deaths increased too.

In recent years, the number of automobile fatalities per year has risen rather than fallen for the first time in decades. Researchers believe that distracted driving due to cell-phone use is a key factor in this troubling increase.

DISTRACTED DRIVING

Distracted driving is not new. In the early 1930s, auto manufacturers began installing radios in cars for the first time. By 1935 an increase in automobile accidents led to a public outcry against the radios. "Ever since auto-radio installations became popular," reported the June 1935 issue of *Radio-Craft* magazine, "a controversy has been going on—between legislative authorities and insurance companies on one hand, and radio manufacturers and car radio owners on the other—as to whether auto radio presented an accident hazard or not."

According to the US Department of Transportation, there are three main types of driver distraction: visual (taking your eyes off the road), manual (taking your hands off the wheel), and cognitive (taking your mind off driving). Twenty-first-century causes of distracted driving include sending a text message while driving, talking on a cell phone, using a navigation system, and eating while driving. The Department of Transportation reported that in 2015, crashes involving a distracted driver killed an average of nine people per day and injured more than one thousand people a day. To improve driver safety, states have begun passing laws about distracted driving. As of 2016, fifteen states; Washington, DC; Puerto Rico; Guam; and the US Virgin Islands have prohibited drivers from using cell phones while in motion.

LOCATIONS IN THE UNITED STATES THAT PROHIBIT DRIVERS FROM USING HANDHELD CELL PHONES

Source: https://www.ghsa.org/state-laws/issues/Distracted-Driving

All drivers prohibited from using handheld cell phones

Some drivers prohibited from using handheld cell phones

*In Arkansas, drivers eighteen to twenty years old are prohibited from using handheld phones while driving.

**In Louisiana and Oklahoma, drivers with learner permits or immediate licenses are prohibited from using handheld phones while driving.

***In New Mexico, drivers in state vehicles are prohibited from using handheld phones while driving.

That number is a jump from 12,155 in 1920 to 50,894 in 1965. Under pressure from consumer advocates such as Ralph Nader, the US Congress decided to act. In 1966 the federal government passed numerous laws, including the National Highway Traffic Safety Act and the National Traffic and Motor Vehicle Safety Act, to address vehicle and traffic safety.

These laws established mandatory basic federal safety standards for motor vehicles. They also created the National Highway Safety Bureau (NHSB), which Congress charged with reducing vehicle-related crashes, saving lives, and preventing injuries. These efforts led to new vehicle safety features including headrests, energy-absorbing steering wheels, shatter-resistant windshields, and mandatory safety belts. They also resulted in changes to highway design such as more visible line stripes, breakaway signs, increased road illumination, and improved barriers to separate traffic lanes.

With so many more cars taking the road, however, a complete end to traffic accidents was nearly impossible. The United States reached a peak number of automobile fatalities in 1973—more than fifty-four thousand. At that time, the number of registered vehicles had climbed to more than 130 million. The United States has taken more precautions since then. State laws mandating seat belt use became common in the 1980s and 1990s. In 1998 a federal law went into effect requiring all cars and light trucks sold in the United States to have airbags on both sides of the front seat. By 2008 auto fatalities had decreased to less than forty thousand in one year.

However, in recent years, auto-accident fatalities have jumped again. The United States saw fewer than thirty-three thousand of these fatalities annually between 2010 and 2014 but more than thirty-five thousand in 2015 and more than thirty-seven thousand in 2016. Government data specialists and other researchers believe that distracted driving is the likely cause—mainly because of cell phone use while driving. The World Health Organization (WHO) is a group that works with nations around the world to combat health hazards and improve living conditions. The organization predicts that based on current trends, auto accidents will pass diseases such as diabetes and tuberculosis to become the number three killer worldwide by the year 2020. These accidents also cost drivers, insurance companies, and local governments more than $300 billion every year, mainly in health-care expenses. Without improvement to car safety, the costs are expected to rise.

CHAPTER TWO

SELF-DRIVING TECHNOLOGY

norman Bel Geddes, RCA, General Motors, and others had exciting visions for autonomous vehicles. But they didn't have the technology necessary to make their vision a reality. That technology came with the development of computers. In the 1960s, many computer scientists at universities and government research organizations realized that developing artificial intelligence (AI) could be key to a self-driving car. AI is the ability of a device to perceive its surroundings and take actions—without human help—to achieve a particular goal. The goal of a self-driving car, for example, would be to move from one point to another as quickly as possible while avoiding obstacles and other vehicles.

A truly self-driving car would not rely on external elements such as radio controls, magnetic strips, or other sensors on the road. Instead, a self-driving car would use its own sensing systems to move through space. Sensing systems would note the car's position on the road and in relation to other objects. Processing systems would understand how best to move around objects and make decisions about speed and direction. And reactive systems would take appropriate actions based on these conditions.

The US government gets involved in researching and designing new technologies of all kinds. For example, the Defense Advanced Research Projects Agency (DARPA)

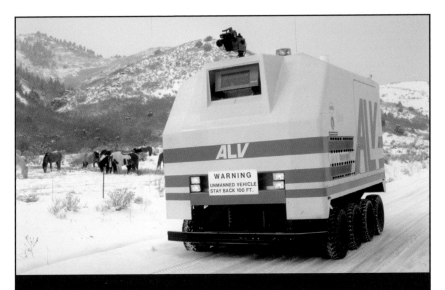

The United States Department of Defense supported research into autonomous driving throughout the 1980s. The Autonomous Land Vehicle (ALV), a product of this research, traveled slowly compared to other automobiles of the time, with the first model reaching speeds of no more than 3 miles (4.8 km) per hour. But it still marked a major development in self-driving technology.

is part of the US Department of Defense. Its main goal is to develop technology that the US military can use. In one notable case, during the 1960s, agency engineers developed communications technology that eventually became the Internet. In 1985 the agency also designed the Autonomous Land Vehicle (ALV), a self-driving vehicle that could move across dangerous territory without an onboard human driver. Agency engineers designed and built the vehicle in just nine months. The result was a 10-foot-tall (3 m) vehicle that resembled a giant ice-cream truck. To provide military personnel with extra security while in battle, the vehicle's system could synchronize with those of other ALVs. This way they could move together in close formation, making an enemy attack more difficult.

In the self-driving car prototypes (models) of the 1980s, sensing and reacting technologies were easy to design. For example, in 1985, the first ALV used a closed-circuit camera to observe its surroundings. The camera would send images to the six computers that controlled the vehicle. The ALV's computers relied on complex algorithms to react to the images and manage the vehicle's controls. However, the computers had trouble processing the information quickly enough to make real-time decisions. As a result, the first ALV could only move at 3 miles (4.8 km) per hour. ALV models built later in the decade could drive themselves at speeds between 19 and 31 miles (31 and 50 km) per hour.

In 1986 a team of engineers at the Robotics Institute at the School of Computer Science at Pittsburgh's Carnegie Mellon University produced a self-driving car prototype as part of its Navlab series. The Navlab 1 could travel at about 20 miles (32 km) per hour on empty city streets with no interference from other vehicles. That year, while working at Bundeswehr University Munich in his native Germany, scientist Ernst Dickmanns designed a vision-guided self-driving van. It drove at 39 miles (63 km) per hour on empty city streets. By 1987 Dickmanns's self-driving van was able to reach speeds of 60 miles (97 km) per hour on empty highways. In 1990 the Navlab 2 reached highway speeds of 70 miles (113 km) per hour.

SPEEDING UP PROCESSING

Despite the advances of engineers across the world, truly autonomous navigation remained a long way off. The biggest challenge was reaction time. The computers that controlled self-driving cars had to process images from a camera quickly enough for a car to react. As one engineer noted, images taken from real-world settings had a lot of visual noise—that is, a huge amount of digital information. The sheer amount of information made it almost impossible for the car's computer systems to identify the important details of an image in a safe amount of time.

Until the late 1980s, most computers were programmed with algorithms that used rule-based programming. Rule-based programming involves "if-then" instructions with numerical conditions before something can take place. Whether or not a condition is met determines the next step in the program until the computer accomplishes its task.

Rule-based programming is good for solving problems that are mathematical or straightforward. However, rule-based calculations were too clunky to handle the large amount of visual information coming from sensors to computer processors in self-driving cars. So, in 1989, Carnegie Mellon's Robotics Institute made an important decision about the processing computers in a new model of its self-driving car. In the next Navlab concept, engineers decided to install computers that relied on an artificial neural network (ANN) to process information from the car's sensors. Engineers hoped that an ANN-based computer could process visual information more efficiently and effectively.

ANNs don't use rule-based programming to process information and make decisions. Their programming

The Robotics Institute at the School of Computer Science at Carnegie Mellon University began work on its Navlab series of self-driving vehicles in 1984 and produced the Navlab 1 (*far left*) in 1986. Four other vehicles followed, Navlab 2–5 (*second from left to far right*). In 1989 the Robotics Institute began to incorporate artificial neural network processing into Navlab vehicles.

instead considers all possible steps and behaviors in a given situation and chooses the best option. ANNs function much the same way as the brains of humans and other animals. In the human brain, small units called neurons transmit electrical signals from one nerve, muscle, or gland cell to another. An ANN is organized in a similar manner, with a collection of connected units called artificial neurons. Each connection can transmit a signal from one artificial neuron to another. The receiving neuron then processes that signal and sends the signal to other neurons. The system efficiently teaches the entire network new tasks and responses to data.

Since the late 1980s, computer engineers have designed ANNs to perform complex tasks that rule-based programming cannot perform. These tasks include speech recognition, image recognition, language translation, imaging for medical diagnoses, and the artificially intelligent engines that power video games. In developing ANNs for self-driving cars, engineers programmed software to guide a car's computer to identify common objects within an image such as potholes and fire hydrants. Artificial neurons were set up to focus on the different features of an image. The neurons would then feed the information to the network to build an image map. The programming could also be set up to prompt a specific behavior in response to certain objects. For example, if the sensor saw a fire hydrant or another obstacle, the computer would prompt the car to avoid it.

Using ANN technology, Carnegie Mellon robotics engineers designed and built the Autonomous Land Vehicle in a Neural Network (ALVINN) in 1989. It was the first self-driving car to use a simple ANN to process information. ALVINN's processor took information from a camera and a laser range finder installed in the car. It then ran the information on an artificial neuron network the engineers had programmed to steer the car in one of forty-six directions based on the information it received. The engineers also designed the ALVINN's network to teach itself which of the different outputs (directions) was best under different road circumstances. The result was a vehicle that could travel through a wooded course at 3.5 miles (5.6 km) per hour—a slow speed by some standards but twice as fast as the vehicle would have traveled without an ANN. In the years afterward, ANNs became the standard processor in self-driving car models.

PROMETHEUS

At about the same time, from 1987 until 1995, a group of eleven European nations were working together to design technology and build components for a self-driving car system. The project was called the Programme for a European Traffic of Highest Efficiency and Unprecedented Safety (Eureka PROMETHEUS). The Eureka member states—Austria, Belgium, Finland, France, Germany, Italy, the Netherlands, Norway, Sweden, Switzerland, and the United Kingdom—contributed nearly $1 billion to universities and car manufacturing companies to do research. The goal was to design a safer, more efficient, more environmentally friendly road traffic system. The early PROMETHEUS vehicles were, like the ALV, very basic. In fact, they could barely function around other traffic and pedestrians. But over time, PROMETHEUS would develop technological improvements in several areas.

NO HANDS
ACROSS AMERICA

In 1995 engineers at Carnegie Mellon University's Robotics Institute decided to send their latest ALVINN model, Navlab 5, on a No Hands across America trip. Navlab 5 was a modified 1990 Pontiac Trans Sport minivan. The engineers outfitted the vehicle with a Sony DXC color video camera and a Sony color LCD (liquid crystal display) monitor. It also had a Trimble Global Positioning System (GPS) and an ANN computer that used a new processing program called Rapidly Adapting Lateral Position Handler (RALPH). RALPH used the video images and the GPS data to determine the conditions of the road ahead and make steering decisions.

The trip began in Pittsburgh , Pennsylvania, and ended in Los Angeles, a distance of nearly 3,000 miles (4,828 km). At times the Navlab 5 reached a top speed of 70 miles (113 km) per hour. For safety reasons, a human operator took control of the car's brakes and throttle when necessary. At the end of the trip, engineers estimated that the car was self-driving for 98.2 percent of the trip.

PROMETHEUS's breakthrough came out of the work of the German robotics engineer Ernst Dickmanns. In the 1980s, Dickmanns led a team of researchers in developing the cameras and other sensors for Mercedes-Benz automobiles. The team's goal was quicker processing of the camera data, with the data then translated into computer commands that could control the steering, throttle, and brakes of the cars.

Starting in 1986, Dickmanns and his team built a series of robot cars. They drove by themselves at speeds of up to 60 miles (97 km) per hour, though only on empty roads. Much like the cars engineers were building at Carnegie Mellon, Dickmanns's robot cars had slow reaction times. The cars' computer systems needed a few seconds to process each camera image, making it difficult for the cars to adjust to other drivers in actual traffic.

Several years after developing his first robot cars, Dickmanns began working with the PROMETHEUS project. One of the partnership's goals was to decrease the time processors needed to analyze the data from camera images. Dickmanns's team developed new methods that translated the visual data in a more efficient way. And to do this, the team copied the way that human eyes record a landscape.

Human eyes don't see a large landscape all at once. With very quick, simultaneous movements, both eyes record small individual details of the landscape. Once the eyes have enough of these details, the human mind fills in the gaps to build an approximate map of the visual landscape. Dickmanns's system utilized this type of saccadic focus (quickly moving between points) in platforms that carried a car's cameras, allowing the cameras to record the most important details of a scene in real time. The cameras recorded image data within milliseconds of seeing something and without relying on previously stored images. This increase in the speed of image processing gave the cars more time to react to road conditions. Dickmanns worked with the PROMETHEUS project for seven years. During this time, their robot cars learned to process various traffic and road conditions more quickly.

VITA

In 1991 the project announced VITA (Vision Information Technology Application). VITA was a Mercedes-Benz van with computer sensors, cameras, and processors, built in cooperation with Daimler AG, the parent company of Mercedes-Benz. One year later, VAMP (Versuchsfahrzeug für autonome Mobilität und Rechnersehen) and VITA II arrived. These vehicles were Mercedes 500SEL cars, outfitted with sensing systems that were more advanced than the first VITA and slightly different from one another. In 1994, in a display of the new technology, VAMP drove in traffic near the busy Charles-de-Gaulle airport in Paris, France, reaching a speed of 80.7 miles (130 km) per hour.

A bolder demonstration came next. In 1995 VAMP received a technological upgrade. It drove from Munich, Germany, to Odense, Denmark, a trip of more than 994 miles (1,600 km). VAMP made 95 percent of the trip without the assistance of an onboard driver. It reached a top speed of 111.8 (180 km) per hour. During the trip, the car safely demonstrated a series of standard driving maneuvers. It passed other cars and changed lanes to the left and right. It also tracked other vehicles as they drove nearby.

INNOVATIONS IN SAFE TECH

In the 1980s and 1990s, new technologies made driving safer. For instance, car manufacturers introduced computerized onboard diagnostic systems. This technology monitors engines and alerts drivers to problems. Onboard diagnostic systems also make cars easier to fix by directing mechanics or car owners toward the problem areas.

In 1991 General Motors introduced its EV1 model car, the first highway-ready, mass-produced fully electric automobile. The battery-powered EV1 model was impractical, however. It could not travel more than 70 to 90 miles (113 to 145 km) on one charge. It cost more to produce, and thus for consumers to buy, than a gasoline-burning car. However, the model still proved that producing a viable electric car was possible.

In 1992 German automobile-part manufacturers Hella and Bosch produced the first low-beam, high-intensity discharge (HID) car headlamps. These headlamps provide better visibility on dark roads than traditional high-beam halogen lamps, offering a greater output of light while requiring less energy. The headlamps were first available on the BMW 7 series of cars. Later, other car manufacturers adopted them on a wide scale.

In 1998, as planned under the Intermodal Surface Transportation Efficiency Act, all automobiles sold in the United States started to be equipped with safe airbags that release during car collisions to cushion passengers. The airbags have led to a significant reduction in the number of yearly traffic fatalities. The next year, Mercedes-Benz introduced radar cruise control systems. They help cars maintain safe distances from other cars, even as the cars change speed. The radar cruise control systems are available in numerous cars made since the start of the 2010s.

GETTING SERIOUS ABOUT SELF-DRIVING

Meanwhile, the US government was also convinced that developing a fully self-driving car was possible. In 1991 the US Congress passed the Intermodal Surface Transportation Efficiency Act (ISTEA). The bill gave the US Department of Transportation the money to design an automated vehicle and highway system by 1997. The bill offered $650 million over six years, not the estimated $40 billion that a full self-driving system would actually require. Even so, it represented a major change in the United States' approach to transportation planning and

In 1997 the National Automated Highway System Consortium (NAHSC) hosted Demo '97, a display of automated highway technology along Interstate 15 in San Diego, California. In this photo, engineer Han–Shue Tan sticks his hands out of the window of a Buick LeSabre as radar and magnetic sensors guide the car forward.

policy. The bill was part of a larger plan to replace the nation's interstate highway system with an intermodal traffic system. The system would include alternative transportation modes such as railroads, bike lanes, and other nonmotorized commuter trails, as well as a self-driving automobile system.

Three years later, the Federal Highway Administration (an agency of the Department of Transportation) created the National Automated Highway System Consortium. The group's goal was to develop what Congress described as a vehicle that allowed for hands-off, feet-off driving. The consortium worked with well-known companies and universities. These partners included Bechtel, a construction company; Caltrans (California Department of Transportation); Carnegie Mellon University; General Motors; Parsons Brinkerhoff, an engineering and design firm; and the University of California, Berkeley.

IT'S MAGIC!

In 1997 the American public got a better look at self-driving technology. The National Automated Highway System Consortium organized a public event to show off the feasibility of an automated highway. Demo '97 featured twenty automated vehicles driving on a stretch of the Interstate 15 highway in San Diego, California. The self-driving cars operated in mixed traffic with a number of non-self-driving vehicles. They also demonstrated platoon driving, in which a line of self-driving cars drive close to one another with coordinated movements.

Observers viewed Demo '97 as a partial success. One writer for the Associated Press went so far as to predict that the consortium's automated highway system would be up and running by 2002. Even so, its funding ran out not long after Demo '97, and the Department of Transportation canceled the program.

Nevertheless, the US government continued to support self-driving research for military use. In 2001, for example, DARPA developed the Demo III vehicle. Much like the earlier ALV, the Demo III could operate in tandem with a group of vehicles. This new vehicle could also drive across miles of difficult terrain while avoiding rocks, trees, and other obstacles.

Spurred by this success, DARPA organized the first Grand Challenge in 2004. This competition offered a prize of $1 million to any self-driving car that could finish a 142-mile (229 km) obstacle course in the Mojave Desert of Southern California. Design and engineering teams

In 2004 the Defense Advanced Research Projects Agency hosted the first of its Grand Challenge events. Engineering teams from around the world entered the competition, in which self-driving prototypes raced one another through an obstacle course in Southern California's Mojave Desert.

from around the world entered the Grand Challenge. No team was able to complete the course, however. In fact, the most successful competitor only managed to go 7.4 miles (12 km). Most of the cars either crashed or their autonomous driving technology could not navigate the rough terrain and unpredictable environment. But the competition signaled how quickly self-driving technology was advancing. In DARPA's Grand Challenge II, held in 2005, five teams finished the course.

"ROBOTICS WOODSTOCK"

On November 3, 2007, DARPA held a new competition—Grand
Challenge III—that came with a twist. Unlike previous challenges
in rugged off-road terrain, this one would take place in a simulated
(mock) city created at the George Air Force Base in Victorville,
California. To win, unmanned ground vehicles (UGVs)—another term
for self-driving cars—would have to complete a 60-mile (97 km)
course through "city" traffic in less than six hours. Competitors'
vehicles had to be able to "merge with traffic, read traffic signs,
navigate roundabouts, busy intersections, and avoid running over
errant [wandering] pedestrians, avoid obstacles—just like a normal
automobile driver."

DARPA offered a $2 million prize to the first car to finish the
course. The agency added $1 million for the second-place finisher
and $500,000 for third place. Self-driving cars from eleven teams
competed in the event, traveling the course while interacting with
fifty other vehicles. Some of these vehicles were also self-driving,
while human drivers occupied others. The "Junior" car developed
by engineers and software designers from Stanford University in
Palo Alto, California, crossed the finish line first, one minute ahead
of Carnegie Mellon's "Boss" car. However, a review of Junior's
traffic violations added enough penalty time to put Boss ahead
as the winner. "That was a galvanizing [exciting] event," said
Carnegie Mellon team member Chris Urmson. "It felt like a robotics
Woodstock [a 1969 music festival that brought together numerous
influential musicians]."

CHAPTER THREE

FROM IF TO WHEN

At the beginning of the twenty-first century, major automobile manufacturers such as Audi, BMW, Ford Motor Company, General Motors, Mercedes-Benz, Nissan, Toyota, Volkswagen, and Volvo got serious about developing and testing self-driving cars. Other self-driving car programs launched in the Netherlands, Italy, and Germany. Ford Motor Company pushed hard. The manufacturer invested in four small high-tech companies that would assist in research and development. Ford's plan was to begin mass-producing self-driving cars in 2021. In 2012 Ford engineers announced that all the technology needed to make viable self-driving cars was in place.

Ford has built research vehicles with high-resolution, omnidirectional cameras that could take images in all

The Ford Motor Company has taken steps toward a viable self-driving vehicle. The company's goal is to mass-produce a self-driving Ford car in its factories by 2021.

directions. The cameras judged surroundings better than any human driver. The vehicles had scanning lasers that could create an instant three-dimensional model of the area around the car. The cars' computers also generated GPS-based maps. Using simultaneous localization and mapping (SLAM) technology, the cars merged data from the cameras and scanning lasers with the GPS maps. New vehicle-to-vehicle communication tools allowed the cars to send out their locations and speeds to one another. The technology on Ford's research vehicles has been able to coordinate the movements of multiple cars as well, a task known as vehicle networking. The company says this technology could be used to control thousands of cars at one time.

The extra sensors and specialized computer processors used in research like this would add thousands of dollars to the price of a car. Initially, most consumers would not be able to afford one. But the public's reluctance to accept self-driving cars might be a greater obstacle. "There is no technology barrier from going where we are now to the autonomous car," said Ford self-driving technology expert Jim McBride. "There are affordability issues, but the big barrier to overcome is customer acceptance." As in the days of the horse and buggy, people are hesitant to give up their familiar form of transportation for a radically new technology.

NEW PLAYER: GOOGLE

In the early twenty-first century, new players entered the scene. One of them was the information technology company Google. It began secretly developing its own self-driving cars in 2009. In early 2010, entrepreneur and computer scientist Sebastian Thrun founded Google X, a research-and-development facility within the company. He led its self-driving car project. Thrun had been on the Stanford University team that finished first in the DARPA Grand Challenge II race in 2005. Google's self-driving car models—at first, modified Toyota automobiles, then modified Lexus sport utility vehicles—used an array of sensors, cameras, radars, and lasers to navigate live traffic. By the end of 2010, Google cars had logged more than 140,000 test miles (225,308 km) on city streets and highways.

In May 2012, Google submitted a modified self-driving Toyota Prius to the Nevada Department of Motor Vehicles for a driver's test through Las Vegas. It would be the world's

SELF-DRIVING CARS 101

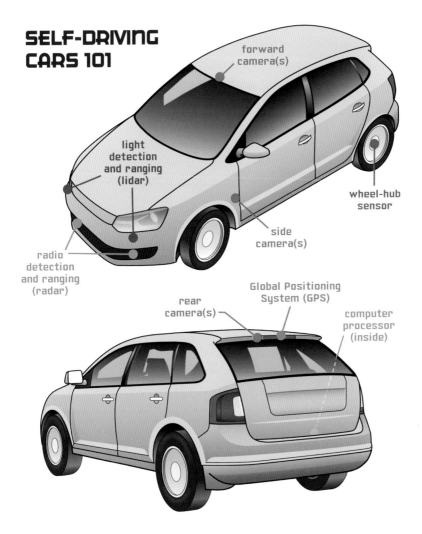

forward camera(s)

light detection and ranging (lidar)

wheel-hub sensor

radio detection and ranging (radar)

side camera(s)

rear camera(s)

Global Positioning System (GPS)

computer processor (inside)

Self-driving cars use multiple forms of technology to access road conditions. In addition to cameras, many rely on lidar (light detection and ranging) technology, which uses pulses of light to measure distance, and radar (radio detection and ranging) technology, which uses radio waves to measure objects' positions and speeds. Features such as lidar, radar, and even a car's main computer processor may be in different parts of a car depending on the model. The number of cameras a self-driving car has may also vary from model to model and from manufacturer to manufacturer.

first official and legal test of a self-driving car. Nevada's DMV allowed Google to choose the route through the city to avoid tricky traffic situations such as roundabouts, railroad crossings, and school zones. The Google car passed the test, even though Google engineers had to take control of the car twice during the drive.

Google was encouraged by the results and in May 2014 announced plans to build one hundred self-driving car prototypes. The engineers of Google's Self-Driving Car Project would design these cars from the ground up, rather than modifying an existing vehicle. "Safety drivers will start testing early versions of these vehicles," the official company blog announced that month. If all went well, the company would provide self-driving vehicles for commuters in California as part of a pilot (test) program. "If the technology develops as we hope, we'll work with partners to bring this technology into the world safely."

NEW PLAYER: TESLA

In October 2014, Tesla Motors made a splash by offering self-driving features for its Model S electric car. Engineer Martin Eberhard and software developer Marc Tarpenning had founded Tesla in 2003. They used start-up money from investor-entrepreneur Elon Musk and several others. In 2008 Musk also assumed the role of Tesla's chief executive officer (CEO). That year Tesla began producing a sports car called the Tesla Roadster.

The Tesla Roadster is the first highway-legal, all-electric production automobile to use small lithium-ion battery cells. The engines of traditional automobiles use a substance like gasoline for fuel. Electric motors are fueled by the chemical energy stored in rechargeable batteries.

MOONSHOT FACTORY

Google calls Google X, its semisecret research-and-development facility, a moonshot factory. The facility, based in Mountain View, California, works to invent and launch game-changing (or moonshot) technologies. Google X teams like to solve big technological challenges through science-fiction-like breakthroughs. The goal is to create products that people can use in everyday life. Among the tools and technologies that Google X teams have worked on are artificial intelligence for speech, language recognition, and visual processing; Android watches; wearable glasses that can compute and communicate; new health-care technologies; and self-driving cars. In 2016 Google X's Self-Driving Car Project graduated from the research facility and became its own company, called Waymo.

In this glimpse of the Google X facility in Mountain View, California, a visitor with legal blindness checks out a self-driving car demonstration.

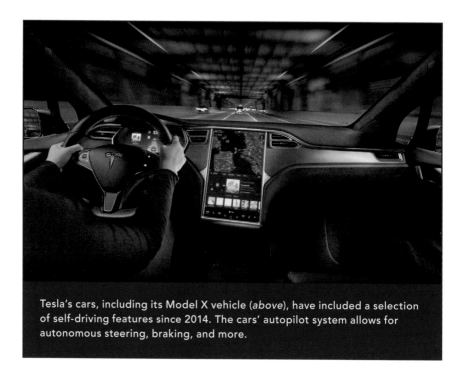

Tesla's cars, including its Model X vehicle (*above*), have included a selection of self-driving features since 2014. The cars' autopilot system allows for autonomous steering, braking, and more.

Tesla's array of battery cells, which the company calls a stack, provides power more efficiently than the large-format battery cells used in other electric cars, and Tesla's cells are cheaper to manufacture too, which helps keep the cost of the car down. The Roadster is also the first production all-electric car that can travel more than 200 miles (322 km) on one charge. In 2012 Tesla replaced the Roadster with the Tesla Model S, a larger, five-door luxury vehicle with autonomous driving features.

Since 2014 Tesla's cars use a new system of sensors and computer controls called Autopilot. This system includes autonomous steering, braking, speed adjustment, and even parking. The system is also able to receive software updates to improve what the car can do. Starting in early 2015, the company began extensive testing of its self-driving technology on a highway between San Francisco, California, and Seattle, Washington. In late 2015, Tesla added a new "summon" feature to the Autopilot software of its cars. This feature allows cars to park themselves without the driver in the car.

"WE SHOULD BE ABLE TO GO ALL THE WAY FROM A PARKING LOT IN CALIFORNIA TO A PARKING LOT IN NEW YORK, NO CONTROLS TOUCHED AT ANY POINT DURING THE ENTIRE JOURNEY."

—Elon Musk, CEO of Tesla

ONLY A MATTER OF TIME

Fully self-driving vehicles are not yet available to the public. However, aspects of self-driving car technology have already reached consumers. Besides Tesla providing autonomous steering in its cars, Mercedes-Benz has also offered several features that make the car partially self-driving. Since 2013 all models of the Mercedes-Benz S-Class car include autonomous steering, sensors to keep the car in its lane, automatic parking, accident avoidance, and driver fatigue detection. All these features function safely at speeds up to 124 miles (200 km) per hour. (At higher speeds, the self-driving features are not reliable.) The same year, Nissan added cameras, radar, and other technologies to its Infiniti Q50 to keep the car in its lane, avoid collisions, and drive the car autonomously for short stretches.

Other traditional automobile manufacturers are including technologies that offer limited self-driving functions. More and more new car models include semiautonomous driving features such as autonomous cruise control, which automatically adjusts a car's speed to maintain a safe distance from other cars; lane assist, which keeps a car positioned in a lane; autonomous parallel parking; and driver fatigue alerts.

By 2014 autonomous features were becoming more common in new cars. So the Society of Automotive Engineers International (SAE) created a classification system that places all cars along a six-part spectrum. At one end of the spectrum are cars with no self-driving features. At the other end are cars with fully autonomous self-driving capabilities. This classification system is based on the amount of driver intervention and attentiveness required, not on the car's capabilities. With this system, SAE aimed to speed the development of a "regulatory framework and best practices to guide manufacturers and other entities in the safe design, development, and deployment of highly automated vehicles." In September 2016, the National Highway Traffic Safety Administration (NHTSA), a part of the US Department of Transportation, adopted the SAE standards.

Companies continue to innovate and refine self-driving technologies. In 2015 and 2016, for example, Volvo tested several hundred self-driving cars from its XC90 series on a 31-mile (50 km) stretch of the city of Gothenberg, Sweden. Each car was equipped with Volvo's autonomous Drive Me technology. By 2017 Volvo tested its XC90 self-driving cars by giving them to one hundred test drivers in China to use on Chinese roads.

LEVELING UP

The Society of Automotive Engineers International, based in the United States, is an organization for engineers across transportation industries. In 2014 the SAE International developed a six-level classification system for automated vehicles. This is how SAE defines each level:

LEVEL 0. No automation. A human driver performs all aspects of driving, including steering, accelerating, decelerating, and monitoring the surrounding environment. A system in the car may issue warning signals but has no vehicle control.

LEVEL 1. Driver assistance (or hands on). An automated system may steer, accelerate, and decelerate the vehicle, or a driver may perform these tasks. The driver still monitors the environment and must be ready to take full control at any time. An example would be adaptive cruise control, in which the driver controls steering and an automated system controls speed.

LEVEL 2. Partial automation (or hands off). An automated system controls steering, accelerating, and decelerating. The driver still monitors the environment and must be ready to take full control at any time.

LEVEL 3. Conditional automation (or eyes off). An automated system controls steering and speed. The system also monitors the surrounding environment. A driver must still be prepared to intervene within a limited time frame if the vehicle issues a warning signal.

LEVEL 4. High automation (or mind off). An automated system controls steering and speed. The system also monitors the surrounding environment. High automation is similar to conditional automation, but a level 4 vehicle must be able to safely park or otherwise end a trip if a driver is unable to retake control after a warning signal.

LEVEL 5. Full automation (wheel optional). An automated system controls all aspects of driving with no human intervention required.

In 2017 Waymo launched its early rider program. This program is an opportunity for participants to experience self-driving cars in action and for Waymo to receive feedback about the performance of its self-driving vehicles. John Krafcik, Waymo's chief executive officer, debuted the program's modified Chrysler Pacifica Hybrid at the 2017 North American International Auto Show in Detroit, Michigan.

By 2020 Volvo engineers hope to have a car that will be fully reliable, posing no safety risks to passengers.

Meanwhile, Google X's Self-Driving Car Project had transformed, becoming a separate company called Waymo underneath Google's parent company, Alphabet. Waymo launched the early rider program in Phoenix, Arizona, in 2017. The test program invites people to apply to become "early riders." These passengers will try out Waymo's self-driving cars to go to places they visit every day such as work, school, or shopping malls. The vehicles are Chrysler Pacifica Hybrid minivans that Waymo has adapted as self-driving cars. They come with test drivers who monitor the vehicles and shut off the self-driving function if necessary. Over the test period, passengers share feedback with Google to help the company improve the cars.

Waymo is not the only company to have launched a recent pilot program to test its self-driving car technology. In 2016 the automobile parts manufacture Delphi and the self-driving-focused software company nuTonomy announced they would collaborate to test six self-driving prototype cars in Singapore.

And since 2016, the transportation company Uber has run test programs using small fleets of self-driving Volvos in Pittsburgh, San Francisco, and Tempe, Arizona. However, Uber's programs have met with setbacks and negative publicity. In February 2017, Waymo filed a lawsuit against Uber, alleging that Uber had utilized technology stolen from Waymo. In March 2017, one of the self-driving

The transportation company Uber has tested vehicles with self-driving technology, such as this modified Volvo, in a select number of American cities.

Volvos in Uber's Tempe program was involved in a collision.

Despite the complex and occasionally contentious race to develop viable self-driving technology on a mass scale, companies continue to make great leaps toward fully self-driving vehicles. In January 2017, new self-driving technology from Audi—the Traffic Jam Pilot, used in its A8 sedan—was the first to receive a SAE level 3 designation. Before that point, most self-driving technologies—BMW's traffic jam assistant, Cadillac's Super Cruise, Mercedes-Benz's Distronic Plus, Tesla's Autopilot, and Volvo's Pilot Assist—had reached SAE level 2 designation. Both Volvo and Audi hope to introduce SAE level 4 self-driving technology in prototype models in 2018. And in June 2017, the release of Tesla's Model 3 vehicle generated new excitement, increasing the public perception that self-driving technology is buzzworthy cool.

CHAPTER FOUR

ROADBLOCKS

Among the greatest expected benefits of self-driving cars is a dramatic reduction in the overall number of traffic accidents and injuries that human error causes each year. According to studies by companies such as Ford and nonprofit safety groups such as the National Safety Council, improper driver behavior causes roughly half of all traffic collisions and fatalities annually. This includes aggressive behaviors such as tailgating and rubbernecking as well as delayed reaction time due to impairment or distraction. In recent years, distracted driving, in particular, has increased as portable communications devices have become more widespread. Video screens and other forms of entertainment technology installed directly into new automobile models also contribute to the problem.

Statistics from the National Safety Council also suggest that driving is becoming more dangerous. In 2015, for instance, traffic fatalities in the United States grew by 7.2 percent, to 35,092 deaths. This was the largest single-year jump in fifty years. Distracted driving was a key factor in this increase. According to one study in Utah, distracted driving caused around 9.4 percent of car crashes annually over an eight-year period. The study showed that accidents caused by distracted driving leaped to almost 20 percent of crashes in 2014.

Another factor adding to the increase in traffic fatalities is excessive speeding, which was responsible for 9,557 fatalities in 2015. According to the National Safety Commission, a company specializing in driver safety solutions, the number of traffic fatalities may have risen as much as 6 percent in the United States in 2016. During

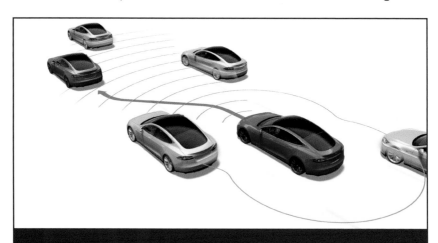

Advocates for self-driving cars believe that an autonomous car's ability to recognize its surroundings and other cars—as demonstrated in this diagram from Tesla—would reduce the number of automobile accidents that take place each year.

that year, traffic accidents also injured an estimated 4.6 million people and resulted in $432 billion in medical costs and property damage. Alcohol is a common factor in these accidents, especially among drivers between the ages of sixteen and twenty. For them alcohol was involved in 37 percent of all traffic deaths in recent years.

Many experts are convinced that self-driving cars could help address these trends. Research suggests that the wide adoption of self-driving cars could eliminate 90 percent of all human-caused automobile accidents in the United States. This reduction would likely prevent up to $190 billion in traffic-related costs. It could also save tens of thousands of lives each year.

BENEFITS FOR EVERYONE

Advocates of self-driving cars say the technology may also bring a reduction in car-related costs. The use of self-driving trucks or other delivery or passenger-carrying vehicles could reduce labor expenses for companies and governments. Driverless deliveries of food or goods would be significantly cheaper, for instance, to the point of possibly transforming commerce. Some companies have already started testing delivery programs that use self-driving technology.

In August 2017, Domino's Pizza announced a pilot program with Ford Motor Company. In a six-week test, Ford Fusion cars with autonomous technology (and an engineer on board) delivered pizzas to Domino's customers in Ann Arbor, Michigan. Domino's used the program to measure customer reactions to driverless delivery. Ford also partnered with several grocery chains to set up test programs for the self-driving delivery

In a six-week test during 2017, Ford Fusion vehicles with autonomous technology delivered food from Domino's Pizza to customers in Ann Arbor, Michigan.

of their goods. And the online retailer Amazon has reportedly been investigating ways to utilize self-driving technology within its delivery services.

Advocates believe that self-driving cars linked to a computer network would better handle the flow of traffic as well, reducing the need for traffic police and road signage. Cars traveling through the traffic system in coordinated groups would theoretically be faster and safer. Increased car safety would mean auto insurance rates would plummet and perhaps even become unnecessary. Meanwhile, people who have long commutes to work could replace hours lost each day to driving in traffic with time for additional work or for leisure activities.

Highways occupied by self-driving cars could safely handle higher speed limits and accommodate more cars spaced more closely together. But the benefits might extend beyond an increase in traffic flow. The widespread use of self-driving cars could mean an overall increase in fuel efficiency and related savings. A system with only self-driving cars also offers huge benefits to urban areas. Widespread use of self-driving cars could lead to more car sharing and reduce the need for parking spaces and lots within a city.

And self-driving cars could change the lives of some people who can't drive. According to a 2017 research paper from the Ruderman Family Foundation, a charitable organization, six million Americans with disabilities have difficulty finding reliable transportation. Nearly 70 percent of these people lack regular employment because of difficulty getting to work. People who have seizures, are elderly or frail, have poor eyesight, or are otherwise impaired in their ability to operate a vehicle would have the same access to cars as anyone else.

Many major cities in the United States are investigating self-driving public transportation. Some are considering introducing autonomous technology into buses and light rails. Experts say the technology has to develop much further to make that possible. But a number of cities around the world—from Ann Arbor and Las Vegas to Helsinki, Finland, and Berlin, Germany—have been testing small numbers of self-driving mass transit vehicles. The French company Navya is a world leader in this field. Navya designed a small, buslike self-driving shuttle that appears in pilot programs around the world.

DRIVING WITH DISSONANCE

The vast majority of drivers in the United States—about 99 percent of them—consider themselves safe drivers despite evidence that they are not. An increasing number of studies show that American drivers exhibit a kind of cognitive dissonance, or a conflict between their beliefs and their behaviors. Their view of themselves as drivers compared to how they actually behave in their cars are at odds. Most drivers regularly engage in unsafe driving practices, according to a recent study by the Ford Motor Company. About 76 percent of American drivers, for example, admitted to eating and drinking beverages while driving. About 55 percent said they regularly drove over the speed limit. About 53 percent admitted they used their cell phones while driving or operated a vehicle when they were drowsy. And 25 percent said they thought there was nothing wrong with picking up a cell phone to search for contact numbers while driving. The survey also found that these reckless driving practices contributed to thousands of accidents or near-accidents among the drivers that they surveyed.

THE SKEPTICISM FACTOR

The widespread use of self-driving cars will always hinge on whether or not human drivers adopt the technology. Many drivers say they don't want to give up control of their cars. They don't want to lose the feelings of power, speed, and freedom that come from driving. Others are skeptical about the safety of self-driving technology, even though studies say self-driving cars would be safer than cars operated by human drivers.

Most drivers have a distorted sense of their own abilities as drivers. A 2011 study from the NHTSA suggested that nearly two-thirds of American drivers rate their driving skills as excellent or very good. However, a large percentage of Americans exhibit risky behaviors when they drive. The study revealed that more than 40 percent of drivers report that they have driven at times at speeds 20 miles (32 km) per hour over the speed limit. And 15 percent of drivers say they have driven while intoxicated. Self-driving technology eliminates risky driving behaviors. Yet many drivers' false sense of their own abilities and decision-making skills makes them less willing to believe that self-driving cars could be safer. Several high-profile accidents have added to people's fears.

In July 2015, Google announced that its self-driving test vehicles had been involved in fourteen minor accidents since 2009. According to project supervisors, however, other human drivers were at fault in thirteen of these fourteen accidents. Eleven incidents had been rear-end collisions that were the fault of drivers in other vehicles. In 2016 Google software caused a crash. The car attempted to avoid sandbags blocking its path and swerved into a bus.

A 2016 collision in Williston, Florida, marked the first traffic fatality involving self-driving technology. In this collision, a Tesla Model S electric car with the Autopilot feature engaged collided with a tractor-trailer.

The first traffic fatality to involve a car using self-driving technology took place in Williston, Florida, during May 2016. A Tesla Model S electric car collided with a large tractor-trailer while in Autopilot mode. According to an investigation by the National Transportation Safety Board (NTSB), a federal agency, the accident happened when the tractor-trailer made a sudden left turn in front of the Tesla at an intersection. The Model S failed to apply its brakes. It struck the trailer and then veered off the road and struck a power pole. The Tesla passenger died at the scene due to injuries from the crash.

In September 2017, after a yearlong investigation, the NTSB concluded that Tesla's Autopilot technology "played a major role" in the crash in Florida because it did not account for improper use by the driver. The board said that Autopilot had performed as intended and the driver of the tractor-trailer did not observe the Tesla. But the fatal collision took place because the Tesla driver deployed the system and turned his attention from the road in conditions that were too dangerous to do so. "The combined effects of human error and the lack of sufficient system controls resulted in a fatal collision that should not have happened," said Robert Sumwalt, the chairperson of the NTSB. The company says that it still expects to offer full self-driving capabilities on its self-driving cars by the end of 2018.

ROADBLOCKS REMAIN

Fear of the unknown is a basic human emotion. In the case of self-driving cars, many people question whether the software can be truly reliable. People worry about whether or not hackers might take control of the cars. People also doubt that artificial intelligence will ever be able to handle the complex and uncertain events that take place on roads. For instance, will self-driving cars operate properly in bad weather? Can they handle random occurrences such as large animals on the road?

Some skeptics believe that advocates for self-driving cars have overstated the technology's benefits. That is, they believe self-driving cars won't be able to function as safely as predicted. And they think the expense of the vehicles limit their benefits. This expense includes not only the cars' purchase price but the costs to maintain and repair the technology as well. It also potentially includes the increased cost of rebuilding and maintaining autonomous highways. And many believe that the benefits of self-driving cars would be unequally distributed—that rich drivers would have access to self-driving technology while people living in poverty would be left behind.

What's more, some people believe that self-driving cars will disrupt and negatively impact city infrastructures and national economies or even the global economy. And once self-driving cars become commercially available, the changes they create in society may be as profound as the one that affected Whip City in the early twentieth century.

Some people believe that an increase in productive travel time and reduced commuting costs will lead people to live farther from cities than they have in recent decades. This would increase travel distances, create more urban sprawl, consume more fuel, and cause further damage to the environment. The question of responsibility for accidents between cars with no drivers is another factor. Before people become more comfortable with self-driving cars, governments will need to create policies and regulations on issues such as these to avoid potential negative impacts from the new technology.

Existing policies in the United States straddle a line between preventing developing self-driving technologies from harming consumers and permitting companies to test their technologies without overly strict regulations. Soon both states and the federal government will have to develop more legislation for issues surrounding self-driving technology. These include standards for safeguards against improper use of the technology, the liability of companies or drivers when a self-driving car is in an accident, and safety standards on car features such as crash protection and braking systems.

TO BUY OR NOT TO BUY

In 2012 J.D. Power and Associates, a market research company, found that 37 percent of Americans would consider purchasing a fully self-driving car. However, that number dropped to just 20 percent when the drivers learned the technology would add $3,000 or more to the cost of the car. Two years later, a survey by Insurance.com revealed that drivers in the United States had become more open to self-driving cars; 75 percent of people surveyed said they would consider buying one. The number rose to 86 percent if owning a self-driving car meant car insurance would be cheaper. Although the interest in self-driving cars grows as companies design newer and more functional car models, fears about the new technology have also grown. Surveys in 2015 and 2016 showed that because of the negative publicity surrounding collisions that involved vehicles with self-driving technology, along with an awareness of the new legal and safety questions the vehicles pose, a significant number of people remained deeply concerned about autonomous driving.

Many critics have asked what a society like the United States will do about the professional driving jobs, automobile insurance positions, and other car-related occupations that will be lost to self-driving cars. The increased use of autonomous vehicles to carry goods would disrupt the labor force. But that disruption will be almost impossible to avoid if self-driving cars become widespread.

The mass adoption of safe, reliable self-driving cars would most likely also cause job losses in public transit services and automobile repair shops. Some estimates suggest that widespread use of self-driving cars could erase up to five million jobs in the United States alone. Despite the increasing excitement about self-driving car technology, for these many reasons, a self-driving future may have serious drawbacks.

Some critics of self-driving cars worry that mass use of these vehicles will increase urban sprawl, similar to this series of roads and housing developments in Mesa, Arizona.

CHAPTER FIVE

THE SELF-DRIVING FUTURE

A 1928 silent film called *Speedy* stars actor Harold Lloyd. It depicts New York City at a time of great transition. The city is "in such a hurry," says one of the film's title cards, that local residents take "Saturday's bath on Friday so they can do Monday's washing on Sunday." In the film, a soda-shop employee named Harold "Speedy" Swift (Lloyd) is in love with Jane Dillon, whose grandfather Pop Dillon operates the city's last horse-drawn trolley. A big modern streetcar company wants to get rid of Pop's trolley so it can continue building mechanized trolley lines. When Pop refuses, the company conspires against him. But Speedy saves the day by organizing a group of local shop owners, mostly elderly, who rely on the old horse-drawn trolley. In the end, the crew forces the streetcar company to give up its schemes and pay Pop $100,000 ($1.4 million in twenty-first-century dollars) for the rights to the old trolley line.

Speedy was a lighthearted comedy. Even so, the story's focus on the horse-drawn trolley reflected people's lingering anxiety during the early days of the automobile. The New York City of 1928 overflowed with trolleys, Model Ts, and other cars rushing chaotically in all directions. And horse-drawn vehicles were struggling to survive in the city's harried streets.

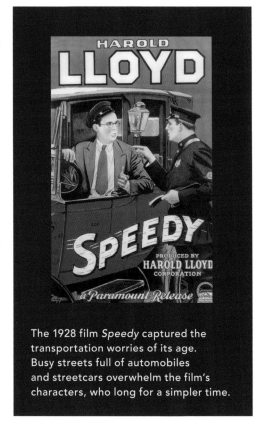

The 1928 film *Speedy* captured the transportation worries of its age. Busy streets full of automobiles and streetcars overwhelm the film's characters, who long for a simpler time.

As the era of the automobile advanced, numerous science-fiction films depicted cars that drove themselves. In the 1990 movie *Total Recall*, set in 2048, action star Arnold Schwarzenegger rode in self-driving taxicabs with mannequin-like robotic drivers. In *Timecop*, a 1994 movie starring martial artist Jean-Claude Van Damme, self-driving cars looked like a cross between a Transformer (a flying car) and a life-size Tonka truck. Passengers in the film controlled the car by giving commands to an intelligent personal assistant much like the iPhone's Siri.

The events in *Timecop* were supposed to take place in 2004. Yet in 2017, more than a decade later and thirty years after DARPA, the Robotics Institute at Carnegie Mellon, and the PROMETHEUS Project built the critical components that make self-driving technology viable, self-driving cars are still not commercially available. It will likely take several decades more before the use of self-driving cars becomes more commonplace.

In the 1990 action film *Total Recall*, characters such as Arnold Schwarzenegger's Douglas Quaid (*in back seat*) ride in self-driving taxis with robotic drivers at the helm.

OLD SCHOOL MEETS NEW SCHOOL

An April 2017 research report by the consulting firm Navigant presented some surprising findings about self-driving cars. Although newer companies such as Waymo, Uber, or Tesla are a part of the race to develop this technology, they may not be in the lead. Rather, the 115-year-old Ford Motor Company is at the forefront.

Navigant's study intended to determine how effective these companies are in making self-driving cars a reality. The firm based its findings on a survey that studied ten criteria such as marketing strategy, production strategy, and product capability. Ford has been testing Fusion Hybrid sedans with autonomous capability on tracks and roads since 2013. It has also developed a number of partnerships with other companies that are developing key self-driving technologies. Ford expects to invest more than $1 billion in self-driving car research before 2021. That year the company plans to begin producing "fully autonomous vehicles."

FUTURE LOOKS

So what will a future filled with self-driving cars really look like? While no one can predict this with absolute accuracy, some possible trends are beginning to develop. Car designers are questioning the need for features such as steering wheels and floor pedals. In a truly self-driving car, neither a steering wheel nor pedals would really be necessary. In fact, Google designed its first self-driving prototype vehicles without these items.

Other designers believe that self-driving car owners will want to hold onto their steering wheels, at least in the short term—to be able to use them in difficult situations

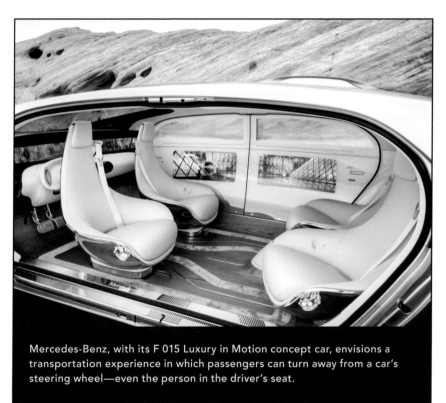

Mercedes-Benz, with its F 015 Luxury in Motion concept car, envisions a transportation experience in which passengers can turn away from a car's steering wheel—even the person in the driver's seat.

that they believe self-driving cars cannot handle. In one 2015 self-driving concept car from Mercedes-Benz, the company's engineers designed a retractable steering wheel. In another, the engineers included a joystick in place of the steering wheel.

Because every person in a self-driving car would be a passenger, designers are rethinking cars' interior spaces. How will people interact with their cars when they are no longer driving them? What will passengers want to do inside their self-driving cars, and how can the cars be designed with this in mind?

Will the interior space become filled with screens—to provide passengers with information, entertainment, and opportunities to work or connect with other people—as with a prototype such as Volvo's Concept 26 car? Or

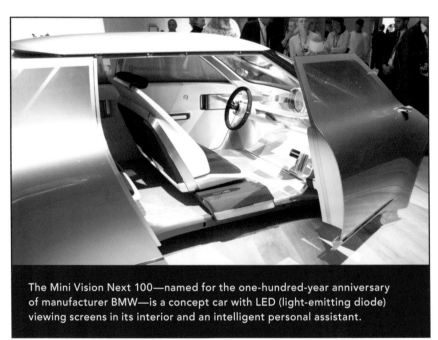

The Mini Vision Next 100—named for the one-hundred-year anniversary of manufacturer BMW—is a concept car with LED (light-emitting diode) viewing screens in its interior and an intelligent personal assistant.

will car interiors become more like lounge spaces, with luxurious sofas on which passengers can relax, escape from the world, and perhaps even sleep as their cars drive them to their destinations—as with the Mercedes F 015 concept car?

"We're asking designers to start with a wider lens, to start with a notion of interaction experiences," said Laura Robin, the director of BMW's Designworks studio in Los Angeles. In October 2016, BMW offered a new vision of a self-driving car with the release of its Mini Vision Next 100 concept car. LED screens covered one side of the passenger cabin, for entertainment viewing or working during a ride. The car also came with its own intelligent personal assistant—not unlike the virtual assistants of *Timecop*'s cars. The assistant could give trip updates or offer other information, such as upcoming appointments. The car could also recognize its owner and acknowledge the person's approach. If multiple people shared the car, the car could recall a person's passenger preferences and prepare itself to the person's liking.

REVOLUTIONIZING HIGHWAYS

The continued emergence of the self-driving car will also transform the highways and cities of the future. In July 2017, the New Jersey Institute of Technology examined future infrastructure needs for cities and highways. The institute proposed a few wild ideas for future highways. One proposal added to road surfaces a photoluminescent (light-emitting) powder to soak up solar light during the day and glow green overnight.

Another idea suggested making roadways out of solar glass panels, LED lights, and microprocessors. The solar panels would heat the roads, reducing the need for snow removal in winter. The LED lights, powered by energy from the solar panels, would light up road lines and symbols while eliminating the need to paint the solar panels. And the microprocessors, also powered by solar energy, could collect traffic and road condition information and keep the system flowing safely.

Optimists suggest that the pairing of self-driving cars and safer, more efficient highways would also transform the terrain of cities and other regions near the roads. Self-driving advocates such as Rob Shirra (the Intelligent Transportation System Society of Canada) and Chris Barker (the C3 Consultancy Group) predict self-driving technology will impact use of space.

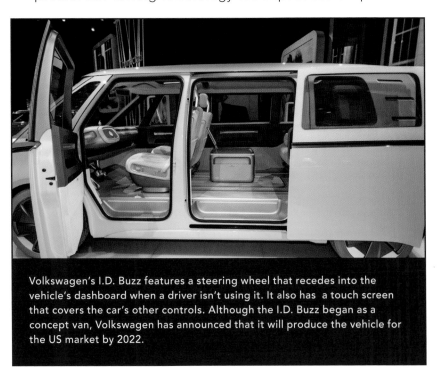

Volkswagen's I.D. Buzz features a steering wheel that recedes into the vehicle's dashboard when a driver isn't using it. It also has a touch screen that covers the car's other controls. Although the I.D. Buzz began as a concept van, Volkswagen has announced that it will produce the vehicle for the US market by 2022.

GOING BEYOND GAMING

Nvidia (pronounced "in-VID-ee-uh"), a tech company based in Santa Clarita, California, is helping accelerate the development of self-driving cars. The company was founded in 1993 to make graphics processing units (GPUs) for the video game industry. GPUs take charge over intense computing functions, such as the graphics in video games. This frees up a central processing unit (CPU) to run the rest of the games' computer code. The technology has allowed the visual details of video games to improve over time without a loss in computing speed. In recent years, Nvidia has led the world in developing the hardware and software that power artificially intelligent computer processors. Volvo, Toyota, and the Chinese company Baidu have all partnered with Nvidia to develop processing platforms for their self-driving cars. Many experts consider Nvidia's Drive PX platforms to be the most dependable artificial-intelligence hardware. It gives self-driving car prototypes the ability to process larger amounts of data, recognize their environment, and navigate roads while maintaining a fast, reliable computing speed.

Cities could then replace these areas with parks, biking trails, gardens, and other green spaces. The result would be much like Norman Bel Geddes envisioned in 1939.

FOUR WHEELS, SIX, OR THREE?

Car users throughout the world are accelerating toward a self-driving future. A 2016 study by *Business Insider* predicted that by the end of 2020, nearly ten million cars with self-driving features would be on the road. These cars would not necessarily all operate at SAE levels 4 or 5. In 2017 no fully autonomous self-driving cars were available for purchase, despite some self-driving technologies in vehicles such as Tesla's Autopilot. Yet some companies are also keeping 2020 in view. Nissan says it is racing to test and perfect a fully self-driving model, with the intent of reaching the market by that year. Other analysts have estimated that fully autonomous (level 5) self-driving cars won't be on the road until around 2030.

Regardless of the year in which self-driving cars take the road in large numbers, they are the likely future of transportation. Steering wheels, traffic jams, and automobile accidents may join buggy whips, manure-strewn streets, and horse-drawn carts as relics of the past. The thought of human-driven cars disappearing from streets may seem unbelievable. But the buggy-whip makers in Whip City never imagined their industry would be replaced.

The only thing limiting the scope of a self-driving future is imagination. Will future cars have four wheels or six or three? Will they be able to predict passenger needs, communicate with the wider traffic system, and conserve fuel to limit emissions? And what will the roadway system look like? Will there be traffic lights? Will the new highways be made of materials that absorb solar energy and help halt the pace of climate change? There's no way to predict the next phase of transportation. Drivers can only be sure, as Norman Bel Geddes once was, that the future of driving will be quite different from the present.

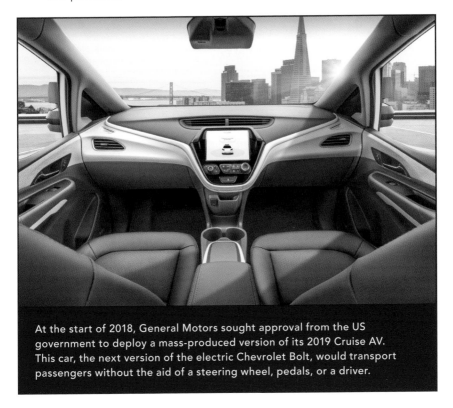

At the start of 2018, General Motors sought approval from the US government to deploy a mass-produced version of its 2019 Cruise AV. This car, the next version of the electric Chevrolet Bolt, would transport passengers without the aid of a steering wheel, pedals, or a driver.

TIMELINE

1478: Artist and engineer Leonardo da Vinci drafts a design for a cart that propels itself through a series of spring mechanisms.

1769: Nicolas Joseph Cugnot builds a working, self-propelled, mechanical land vehicle. The Automobile Club of France and the British Royal Automobile Club later recognize the vehicle as the world's first automobile.

1808: François Isaac de Rivaz builds the first internal-combustion automobile. The vehicle uses a hydrogen-powered internal combustion engine.

1885: Karl Benz designs the Benz Patent-Motorwagen, the first successful production automobile.

1908: Henry Ford and Ford Motor Company release the Model T car, marking a shift in the affordability of automobiles.

1913: A Ford Motor Company factory installs the first moving assembly line, increasing the efficiency with which the company produces cars.

1925: Engineer Francis P. Houdina holds a demonstration in which he directs a car using radio signals. The car, a Chandler automobile fixed with an antenna, goes off course.

1939: Designer Norman Bel Geddes unveils his Futurama exhibit at the World's Fair in New York City. Futurama displays his vision of an autonomous highway, later covered in the book *Magic Motorways*.

1956: President Dwight D. Eisenhower signs the Federal-Aid Highway Act, prompting the construction of the US interstate highway system.

1958: The Radio Corporation of America begins to test technology designed to support an automatic highway system, with mixed results.

1966: In response to concerns about vehicle safety, the US federal government passes laws such as the National Highway Traffic Safety Act and the National Traffic and Motor Vehicle Safety Act.

1985: The Defense Advanced Research Projects Agency (DARPA) designs the Autonomous Land Vehicle (ALV). This vehicle can cross rough territory without an onboard human driver.

1986: The Robotics Institute at the School of Computer Science at Carnegie Mellon University creates the first entry in its Navlab series of self-driving prototypes, Navlab 1.

1987: Eleven European nations found the Programme for a European Traffic of Highest Efficiency and Unprecedented Safety (Eureka PROMETHEUS), a cooperative effort to design and build new self-driving technology.

1989: The Robotics Institute at Carnegie Mellon University begins to utilize an artificial neural network (ANN) in its self-driving prototypes, a practice that later becomes the standard.

1995: VAMP (Versuchsfahrzeug für autonome Mobilität und Rechnersehen), a Mercedes 500SEL car outfitted with state-of-the-art computer sensors and camera systems, drives a length of more than 994 miles (1,600 km) between Munich, Germany, and Odense, Denmark.

1997: The National Automated Highway System Consortium hosts Demo '97, a public demonstration of self-driving technology on the Interstate 15 highway in San Diego, California.

2004: The Defense Advanced Research Projects Agency organizes the first of its Grand Challenge events, a series of competitions between teams of self-driving car engineers.

2009: Google founds its Google X research-and-development facility, the hub of its research into self-driving vehicle technology for the next several years.

2014: Tesla Motors begins to offer Autopilot in all of its vehicles. This system of sensors and computer controls allows for autonomous steering, braking, speed adjustment, and parking.

The Society of Automotive Engineers International (SAE) introduces its six-part classification system for cars based on their self-driving features.

2016: The first fatality involving a car with autonomous technology takes place in Williston, Florida, as a Tesla Model S collides with a tractor-trailer.

2017: Waymo begins its Early Rider Program, an opportunity for volunteers in Phoenix, Arizona, to ride in adapted, self-driving Chrysler Pacifica Hybrid minivans.

Ford Motor Company and Domino's Pizza test driverless meal deliveries in Ann Arbor, Michigan, in an effort to measure customer responses to the new technology.

2018: Speakers at the International Consumer Electronics Show in Las Vegas share new developments in self-driving technology, including Nvidia's Drive Xavier processor, which the company has designed to direct autonomous taxis.

General Motors seeks approval from the US Department of Transportation to launch its self-driving 2019 Cruise AV.

SOURCE NOTES

11   John T. Jost, "Resistance to Change: A Social Psychological
     Perspective," *Social Research* 83, no. 3 (Fall 2015): 607.

15   "1908: Ford Motor Company Unveils the Model T," History.com,
     accessed August 1, 2017, http://www.history.com/this-day-in
     -history/ford-motor-company-unveils-the-model-t.

21   "Radio-Driven Auto Runs Down Escort," *New York Times*, July 28,
     1926.

22   Norman Bel Geddes, *Magic Motorways* (New York: Random House,
     1940), 10.

23   Ibid. 3.

23   Ibid. 4.

23   Daniel Bartz, "Autonomous Cars Will Make Us Safer," *Wired*,
     November 16, 2009, https://www.wired.com/2009/11/autonomous
     -cars/.

26   "National Interstate and Defense Highways Act (1956) Document
     Info," Our Documents, accessed October 26, 2017, https://www
     .ourdocuments.gov/doc.php?flash=false&doc=88.

29   "Highway of the Future," *Electronic Age*, January 1958, 12.

30   Don Quigg, "Reporter Rides Driverless Car," *Oxnard (CA) Press-
     Courier*, June 7, 1960.

32   Matt Novak, "Distracted Drivers Are Nothing New," *Pacific
     Standard*, February 21, 2013, https://psmag.com/environment/the
     -1930s-battle-over-car-radios-and-distracted-driving-52823.

51   "Urban Challenge," DARPA, accessed July 15, 2017, http://archive
     .darpa.mil/grandchallenge/.

51   Ibid.

54   Kevin Fitchard, "Ford Is Ready for the Autonomous Car. Are
     Drivers?," *Gigaom.com*, April 9, 2012, https://gigaom.com
     /2012/04/09/ford-is-ready-for-the-autonomous-car-are-drivers/.

56   "Just Press Go: Designing a Self-Driving Vehicle," *Google* (blog),
     May 27, 2014, https://googleblog.blogspot.com/2014/05/just-press
     -go-designing-self-driving.html.

56   Ibid.

59   "The Future We're Building—and Boring," TED, accessed
     November 17, 2017, https://www.ted.com/talks/elon_musk_the_
     future_we_re_building_and_boring.

60 "U.S. Department of Transportation's New Policy on Automated Vehicles Adopts SAE International's Level of Automation for Defining Driving Automation in On-Road Motor Vehicles," SAE International, September 22, 2016, https://www.sae.org/news/3544/.

73 Neal E. Boudette and Bill Vlasic, "Tesla's Self-Driving System Faulted by Safety Agency in Crash," *New York Times*, September 12, 2017.

77 *Speedy*, directed by Ted Wilde (Hollywood, CA: Paramount Pictures, 1928).

80 Alexandra Simon-Lewis, "Ford Is the Leading Self-Driving Car Manufacturer—Ahead of Waymo, Tesla and Uber," *Wired*, April 4, 2017, http://www.wired.co.uk/article/ford-autonomous-cars-navigant-leader.

83 Matt Bubbers, "Reinventing the Wheel," *Globe and Mail* (London), last modified November 3, 2016, https://www.theglobeandmail.com/globe-drive/what-the-self-driving-shareable-electric-cars-of-the-future-will-look-like/article32643416/.

GLOSSARY

algorithm: a process, or a system of rules, that determines how a computer solves a problem

artificial intelligence (AI): the ability of a machine to imitate intelligent human behavior. Computers with artificial intelligence can accomplish goals such as learning, planning, problem solving, and speech recognition.

artificial neural network (ANN): a computing system that imitates the biological neural networks of animal brains. Within an artificial neural network, connected units called artificial neurons send signals to one another or process the signals.

buggy whip: a horsewhip used by drivers of horse-drawn vehicles such as horses and buggies, carriages, stagecoaches, and sleighs to control the speed and direction of the horses

cog track: a mechanical system that uses cogs or pinions (small gear wheels) within a track to move a vehicle forward. Cog track systems most often propel locomotive trains, especially on tracks that cover steep slopes.

concept car: a model of car, or prototype, created to demonstrate a new style or technology in automobile design. Concept cars do not go directly into production. They are the starting point for a car design that will develop further until it is practical, safe, and affordable.

constructive disruptive technology: a term used since the 1990s to describe a balance between the development of a technology that displaces an established technology and shakes up society—and a slower approach to technological change that takes into account a society's existing systems

consumer culture: a culture within a modern capitalist society centered on selling consumer goods—such as appliances, cars, clothes, and media—and spending consumer money

Defense Advanced Research Projects Agency (DARPA): an agency of the US Department of Defense (DOD), founded in February 1958 as the Advanced Research Projects Agency. DARPA develops new technologies for the US military.

electric ignition: a system in internal combustion engines and similar devices that generates a spark to ignite a mixture of fuel and air. The most common use of electric ignition is in vehicles with gasoline-burning engines, such as cars, buses, motorcycles, trucks, and vans.

graphics processing unit (GPU): a specialized electronic processor that accelerates the creation of graphic images or video images for a device designed to display them. Graphics processing units are used in computer-aided design programs, engineering programs, geographic information systems, and self-driving cars.

horseless carriage: an early term for the automobile

infrastructure: physical structures, such as roads, buildings, sewers, lights, and other physical systems or items, that keep cities and communities running smoothly and safely

internal combustion engine: a type of engine that burns fuel in a small space called a combustion chamber. Hot gases expand in the chamber and cause pistons or rotors to move. Together the movement and the fuel power a vehicle or machine.

lidar: light detection and ranging technology, which uses pulses of light to measure distance

moving assembly line: a manufacturing process in which the parts of a complex product, such as a car or an appliance, travel along a moving platform to successive workstations. At each station, an assembler adds a part to the product. This process makes assembling an entire product quick and easy.

omnidirectional: oriented toward or receiving signals from all directions

onboard diagnostic system: a system of computer processors that gives vehicle owners and repair technicians information about the various working parts of a vehicle. An onboard diagnostic system can identify vehicle parts or systems that are not working properly.

parent company: a company that has control and ownership of other, smaller companies

prototype: the first model of a machine, vehicle, or other device, often for testing or demonstrations

radar: radio detection and ranging technology, which uses radio waves to measure the positions and speeds of objects

saccadic movement: a quick, jerky, simultaneous movement of both eyes from one position to another. Humans and some animals do not typically process a scene or image by fixing their eyes on it. Instead, their eyes move around between different parts of a scene to build a three-dimensional map of the scene.

simultaneous localization and mapping (SLAM): a form of navigation technology that creates a computer map of an unknown environment while also monitoring the vehicles that are in that environment.

vulcanized rubber: a type of rubber that has been treated by a chemical process known as vulcanization. This process converts natural rubber (which is a liquid sap) into a solid, stretchy, and more durable material by adding sulfur or similar chemicals to the sap.

SELECTED BIBLIOGRAPHY

Ackerman, Evan. "Self-Driving Cars Were Just around the Corner—in 1960." *Institute of Electrical and Electronic Engineers Spectrum*, August 31, 2016. http://spectrum.ieee.org/geek-life/history /selfdriving-cars-were-just-around-the-cornerin-1960.

———. "Study: Intelligent Cars Could Boost Highway Capacity by 273%." *Institute of Electrical and Electronic Engineers Spectrum*, September 4, 2012. http://spectrum.ieee.org/automaton/robotics /artificial-intelligence/intelligent-cars-could-boost-highway -capacity-by-273.

Bartz, Daniel. "Autonomous Cars Will Make Us Safer." *Wired*, November 16, 2009. https://www.wired.com/2009/11/autonomous-cars/.

Bel Geddes, Norman. *Magic Motorways*. New York: Random House, 1940.

Bellis, Mary. "Who Invented the Car?" *ThoughCo.* Last modified July 1, 2016. https://www.thoughtco.com/who-invented-the-car-4059932.

Bubbers, Matt. "Reinventing the Wheel." *Globe and Mail* (London). Last modified November 3, 2016. https://www.theglobeandmail.com /globe-drive/what-the-self-driving-shareable-electric-cars-of-the -future-will-look-like/article32643416/.

Chung, Emily. "Self-Driving Cars: 5 Ways They Could Change City Life." *CBC News*, May 22, 2015. http://www.cbc.ca/news/technology/self -driving-cars-5-ways-they-could-change-city-life-1.3082638.

Curcio, Vincent. *Henry Ford*. New York: Oxford University Press, 2013.

Darrow, Barb. "Distracted Driving Is Now an Epidemic in the U.S." *Fortune*, September 14, 2016. http://fortune.com/2016/09/14 /distracted-driving-epidemic/.

Dudley, David. "The Driverless Car Is (Almost) Here." *AARP the Magazine*, December 2014/January 2015. https://www.aarp.org /home-family/personal-technology/info-2014/google-self-driving -car.html.

Fitchard, Kevin. "Ford Is Ready for the Autonomous Car. Are Drivers?" *Gigaom.com*, April 9, 2012. https://gigaom.com/2012/04/09/ford-is -ready-for-the-autonomous-car-are-drivers/.

Flink, James J. *The Automobile Age*. Cambridge, MA: MIT Press, 1988.

Fox, Justin. "The Great Paving: How the Interstate Highway System Helped Create the Modern Economy—and Reshaped the Fortune 500." *Fortune*, January 26, 2004, 77–84.

Geier, Ben. "Tim Cook Says Apple Is Working on Self-Driving Tech: Just Not a Car." *CNN*, June 13, 2017.

"The Great Smog of 1952." *Met Office*. Accessed August 17, 2008. http://www.metoffice.gov.uk/learning/learn-about-the-weather /weather-phenomena/case-studies/great-smog.

Harris, Mark. "How Google's Autonomous Car Passed the First U.S. State Self-Driving Test." *Institute of Electrical and Electronic Engineers Spectrum*, September 10, 2014. http://spectrum.ieee .org/transportation/advanced-cars/how-googles-autonomous-car -passed-the-first-us-state-selfdriving-test.

"Highway of the Future." *Electronic Age*, January 1958, 12–14.

Jost, John T. "Resistance to Change: A Social Psychological Perspective." *Social Research* 83, no. 3 (Fall 2015): 607–636.

"Just Press Go: Designing a Self-Driving Vehicle." *Google* (blog), May 27, 2014. https://googleblog.blogspot.com/2014/05/just-press-go -designing-self-driving.html.

Kendall, Marisa. "How Nvidia's 'Brains' Are Dominating the Self-Driving Car Race." *Minneapolis Star Tribune*, July 16, 2017. http://www .startribune.com/how-nvidia-s-brains-are-dominating-the-self -driving-car-race/434582273/.

Korosec, Kirsten. "2016 Was the Deadliest Year on American Roads in Nearly a Decade." *Fortune*, February 15, 2017. http://fortune .com/2017/02/15/traffic-deadliest-year.

———. "U.S. Traffic Deaths Make the Biggest Leap in 50 Years." *Fortune*, August 29, 2016. http://fortune.com/2016/08/29/us-traffic -deaths-tech/.

Lorenzi, Rossella. "Da Vinci Sketched an Early Car." *News in Science*, April 26, 2004. http://www.abc.net.au/science/news/stories /s1094767.htm.

Lowensohn, Josh. "This Is Tesla's D: An All-Wheel Drive Model S with Eyes on the Road." *Verge*, October 9, 2014. https://www.theverge .com/2014/10/9/6955357/this-is-tesla-s-d-an-a.

Melosi, Martin V. "The Automobile and the Environment in American History." *Automobile in American Life and Society*. Accessed July 1, 2017. http://autolife.umd.umich.edu/Environment/E_Overview/E_ Overview4.htm.

Novak, Matt. "Distracted Drivers Are Nothing New." *Pacific Standard*, February 21, 2013. https://psmag.com/environment/the-1930s -battle-over-car-radios-and-distracted-driving-52823.

Oagana, Alex. "A Short History of Mercedes-Benz Autonomous Driving Technology." *autoevolution*, January 25, 2016. https://www. autoevolution.com/news/a-short-history-of-mercedes-benz -autonomous-driving-technology-68148.html.

Pomerleau, Dean. "ALVINN: An Autonomous Land Vehicle in a Neural Network." *Advances in Neural Information Processing Systems*. San Francisco: Morgan Kaufmann, 1980.

Reid, Keith. "Happy Days: For Petroleum Marketers, the 1950s Lived Up to the Nostalgia." *National Petroleum News*, June 2004, 24–25.

Rettinger, Jonathan. "How Close Are We to a Real Self-Driving Car?" *Huffington Post*, October 21, 2015. http://www.huffingtonpost.com /jonathan-rettinger/how-close-are-we-to-a-rea_b_8346966.html.

Setright, L. J. K. *Drive On! A Social History of the Motor Car.* London: Granta Books, 2003.

Strahan, Derek. "Whip Factories on Elm Street, Westfield, Mass." *Lost New England*. Accessed August 1, 2017. http://lostnewengland .com/category/massachusetts/westfield-massachusetts.

Tegethoff, Eric. "Report: Self-Driving Cars Could Improve Lives of People with Disabilities." *Public News Service*, January 26, 2017. http://www .publicnewsservice.org/2017-01-26/disabilities/report-self-driving -cars-could-improve-lives-of-people-with-disabilities/a56082-1.

"Tesla's Elon Musk Expects Self-Driving Cars in 3 Years." *USA Today*. Last modified June 9, 2015. https://www.usatoday .com/story/money/cars/2015/06/09/elon-musk-tesla-self -driving/28766805/?utm_source=huffingtonpost.com&utm_ medium=referral&utm_campaign=pubexchange_article.

Thiel, Wade. "The VaMoRs Was the World's First Real-Deal Autonomous Car." *Web2carz.com*, February 28, 2017. http://www.web2carz.com /autos/car-tech/6396/the-vamors-was-the-worlds-first-real-deal -autonomous-car.

Wang, Ucilia. "Self-Driving Cars Are Coming, and the Technology Promises to Save Lives." *Guardian* (London), December 17, 2015. https://www.theguardian.com/technology/2015/dec/17/self-driving -cars-safety-future-interactive.

Williams, Matt. "What Are the Uses of Electromagnetics?" *Universe Today*. Last modified January 13, 2016. https://www.universetoday .com/39295/uses-of-electromagnets.

Yvkoff, Liane. "Many Car Buyers Show Interest in Autonomous Car Tech." *CNET*, April 27, 2012. https://www.cnet.com/roadshow/news/many -car-buyers-show-interest-in-autonomous-car-tech.

FURTHER INFORMATION

Books

Humes, Edward. *Door to Door: The Magnificent, Maddening, Mysterious World of Transportation*. New York: Harper, 2016. Pulitzer Prize–winning journalist Edward Humes explores the unseen complexities of how people and goods travel in contemporary society. Humes draws on data, interviews, and his own family's experiences to reveal what everyday events such as traffic jams and grocery runs reveal about the current state and future of transportation.

January, Brendan. *Information Insecurity: Privacy under Siege*. Minneapolis: Twenty-First Century Books, 2016. As the computing power contained in cars grows stronger, and cars can increasingly tailor their settings to a driver's preferences, questions of data security are on the minds of many drivers. In *Information Insecurity*, January explores the process of electronic data collection, including its uses and its controversies. Find out who is tracking us, how they are tracking us, and what they are doing with the information they compile.

Koch, Melissa. *3D Printing: The Revolution in Personalized Manufacturing*. Minneapolis: Twenty-First Century Books, 2018. Another disruptive technology, 3D printing, putting the power to produce complex goods into the hands of individual makers. Learn about the history of 3D printing technology, key materials, and popular uses. Koch interviews industry leaders, examines questions surrounding 3D printing's environmental impact, and more.

Lipson, Hod, and Melba Kurman. *Driverless: Intelligent Cars and the Road Ahead*. Cambridge, MA: MIT Press, 2016. In this book, Lipson and Kurman give readers an accessible overview of the disruptive technology behind self-driving cars. They also consider the possible impacts, pros and cons, of the technology and advocate for a cultural shift toward accepting self-driving cars.

McPherson, Stephanie Sammartino. *Artificial Intelligence: Building Smarter Machines*. Minneapolis: Twenty-First Century Books, 2018. Smart cars, space robots, and drones. How did we get here? Award-winning author Stephanie Sammartino McPherson explores the history and development of AI from the mid-1950s onward. Meet industry pioneers and leaders, learn about the sciences of AI and neurology, consider the ethics of AI, and discover what lies ahead.

Mueller, John Paul, and Luca Massaron. *Artificial Intelligence for Dummies*. Hoboken, NJ: Wiley, 2018. This book in the For Dummies series provides a clear guide to the technology that makes self-driving cars possible. Learn about the uses of artificial intelligence, its limits, common misconceptions, and more.

Tillemann, Levi. *The Great Race: The Global Quest for the Car of the Future*. New York: Simon & Schuster, 2015. Who will control the future of the car? In this book, readers will learn more about the state of the automobile industry in the twenty-first century, including the latest technological advances. Tillemann describes where the United States, China, and Japan each fit within the industry and as competitors for industry dominance.

Vance, Ashlee. *Elon Musk and the Quest for a Fantastic Future*. New York: Harper, 2017. This biography of entrepreneur Elon Musk takes young adult readers along Musk's journey from South Africa to the United States and traces his push for innovation in transportation, space, and energy.

Websites

BrainPOP: Cars
https://www.brainpop.com/technology/transportation/cars
BrainPOP's car site helps visitors unpack the complex technology that powers modern cars, with aids including activities, games, movies, and more.

History: Automobile History
http://www.history.com/topics/automobiles
This website from the History Channel provides an online record of important events in the development of the automobile. Check out informative videos, famous speeches, articles about the evolution of the car, and more.

Nissan Blog: Nissan's Self-Driving Car
https://www.nissanusa.com/blog/autonomous-drive-car
This piece from the Nissan Motor Company blog outlines Nissan's plan to put self-driving cars on the road by 2020. Take a look at Nissan's development process, and learn more about the company's approach to intelligent mobility.

Science News: Five Challenges for Self-Driving Cars
https://www.sciencenews.org/article/five-challenges-self-driving-cars
This diagram-packed article gives different experts the chance to sound off on the last roadblocks to the success of self-driving cars, including cybersecurity hazards, ethical questions, and the complications of human-robot interaction.

TED: Driverless Cars

https://www.ted.com/topics/driverless+cars

In this collection of TED Talks on the topic of driverless cars, social scientist Iyad Rahwan considers the decisions self-driving cars should make, roboticist Chris Urmson explains how self-driving cars see the road, and other experts deliver talks on the many questions surrounding self-driving cars and artificial intelligence.

Tesla Autopilot

https://www.tesla.com/autopilot

Tesla's Autopilot provides full self-driving hardware on all Tesla cars. Discover more information about this technology, including the range of its cameras, the scope of its processing power, and examples of its use in everyday driving situations.

Volvo Intellisafe

https://www.volvocars.com/au/about/innovations/intellisafe

Intellisafe, the autonomous driving technology of Volvo Cars, gives drivers autonomous breaking, a Lane Keeping Aid, and more. This site has footage of cars with Intellisafe technology in action and details about Volvo's future plans.

Waymo

https://waymo.com

Waymo is working toward fully self-driving cars that make it safe and easy for people to get around. The Waymo site profiles participants in Waymo's early riders program, traces the increase in miles driven by Waymo's self-driving fleet, and explains Waymo technology with videos and diagrams.

INDEX

ABOUT THE AUTHOR

Michael Fallon is a writer based in Minnesota. He has published pieces in dozens of magazines, journals, and newspapers. He is also the author of two books about the cultural history of the 1970s and three young adult books on topics such as art and family. Fallon has a wide range of interests including sports, visual art, science and technology, crafts, American history, science fiction, music, food, childhood, fatherhood, and many more. Personally, he can hardly wait for the era of self-driving cars, so he can give up driving and catch up on his reading. Find him at http://www.writermichaelfallon.com.

PHOTO ACKNOWLEDGMENTS

The images in this book are used with the permission of: DKart/E+/Getty Images, p. 1; Holyoke History Room of the Holyoke Public Library, p. 5; The British Library/flickr.com/(Public Domain), p. 6 (top); © Derek Strahan, p. 6 (bottom); Science & Society Picture Library/Getty Images, p. 7; Joe deSousa/Wikimedia Commons (CC0 1.0), p. 9; Bettmann/Getty Images, p. 10; The Granger Collection, New York, p. 11; Library of Congress (LC-USZ62-19261), p. 13; Pierre Poschadel/Wikimedia Commons (CC BY-SA 3.0), p. 14; The Advertising Archives/Alamy Stock Photo, p. 17; Alfred Eisenstaedt/The LIFE Picture Collection/Getty Images, p. 21; National Archives, p. 25; PhotoQuest/Archive Photos/Getty Images, p. 27; Daxiao Productions/Shutterstock.com, p. 31; Laura Westlund/Independent Picture Service, pp. 33, 55; Bill Pierce/The LIFE Images Collection/Getty Images, p. 37; Firefly4342/Wikimedia Commons (CC BY-SA 4.0), p. 40; Bob Grieser/Los Angeles Times/Getty Images, p. 47; Gina Ferazzi/Los Angeles Times/Getty Images, p. 49; Ford Motor Company, pp. 53, 68; Kim Kulish/Corbis News/Getty Images, p. 57; Tesla Motors, pp. 58, 66; Bill Pugliano/Getty Images, p. 62; Dllu/Wikimedia Commons (CC BY-SA 4.0), p. 63; National Transportation Safety Board/Florida Highway Patrol investigators/flickr.com (CC0 1.0), p. 72; Tim Roberts Photography/Shutterstock.com, p. 76; RGR Collection/Alamy Stock Photo, p. 78; AF archive/Alamy Stock Photo, p. 79; Courtesy of Mercedes-Benz USA, LLC, p. 80; Stephen Hardman/Getty Images, p. 82; Steve Lagreca/Shutterstock.com, p. 84; General Motors, p. 87; Artizarus/Shutterstock.com (Wi-Fi icon); Bardocz Peter/Shutterstock.com (map background); -VICTOR-/DigitalVision/Getty Images (car icons).

Cover: DKart/E+/Getty Images; Artizarus/Shutterstock.com (Wi-Fi icon); -VICTOR-/DigitalVision/Getty Images (car icons); Bardocz Peter/Shutterstock.com (map background).